"With wonderful insight and clarity, Wayne Mack explores the difficult issue of how to reconcile God's justice with His sovereignty. He shines the bright light of Scripture on some of the toughest questions of all and then carefully explores the answers in a way that is easy to follow and truly helpful."

—JOHN MACARTHUR, pastor, Grace Community Church; founder, *Grace to You* radio program

"*It's Not Fair!*' is a simple yet profound and practical book. Since we are all prone to murmur against God's kind providence, everyone should read this book. Like the book of Job, *It's Not Fair!*' moves us from a disgruntled spirit to end in God and His glorious attributes."

—JOEL R. BEEKE, president, Puritan Reformed Theological Seminary, Grand Rapids

"Wayne points the reader to God by surveying His attributes, not merely in the abstract, but as practical comfort for hurting souls. He expounds Scripture while effectively weaving in biblical examples and real-life cases from his vast experience as a counselor. The applications are direct and specific."

—JIM NEWHEISER, director of Institute for Biblical Counseling and Discipleship, Grace Bible Church, Escondido, California

"*It's Not Fair!*' is an honest assessment of how we have allowed contemporary notions of fairness to rule our hearts rather than coming to grips with the true nature of God and His character. By helping us to see the actual God of the Bible, the authors provide tremendous insight in our understanding of how to grapple with the genuine pain and vexing challenges of the Christian life."

—LANCE QUINN, pastor and teacher, The Bible Church of Little Rock

"Who hasn't complained that life is unfair? Wayne Mack analyzes that common complaint from a biblical and heavenly perspective, reminding us why we don't really want what's 'fair.'"

—PHIL JOHNSON, executive director,
Grace to You radio program

"In contrast to the plethora of self-help books that point you inside your despairing self for an answer to the nightmares of life, Wayne Mack has written a book that points you away from yourself to the God who ordains all things. The cry, 'It's not fair!' will give way to 'wonder, love, and praise.'"

—CONRAD MBEWE, pastor, Kabwata Baptist Church,
Lusaka, Zambia

"In writing *'It's Not Fair!'*, Dr. Mack has once again put into our hands a book that will train us to think God's way and to compel us, even when we are in the mire of life, to come to the conclusion that 'it is fair.' I highly commend it!"

—RONALD KALIFUNGWA, pastor,
Lusaka Baptist Church, Zambia

"Some Christian books are like bad soup—thin, watery, and lacking in nutritional value. In contrast, *'It's Not Fair!'* is like a good stew—thick, meaty, and spiritually sustaining. As with all of Wayne Mack's books, this one is so packed with Bible you'll need to eat it with a fork, not a spoon. Enjoy!"

—JOEL JAMES, pastor, Grace Fellowship Church,
Pretoria, South Africa

"IT'S NOT FAIR!"

Finding Hope When Times Are Tough

WAYNE A. MACK

WITH

DEBORAH HOWARD

P U B L I S H I N G

P.O. BOX 817 • PHILLIPSBURG • NEW JERSEY 08865-0817

Page design by Kirk DouPonce, DogEared Design

Printed in the United States of America

Library of Congress Cataloging-in-Publication Data

Mack, Wayne A.
"It's not fair!" : finding hope when times are tough / Wayne A. Mack with Deborah Howard.
 p. cm.
Includes bibliographical references and index.
ISBN 978-1-59638-112-4 (pbk.)
1. Providence and government of God—Christianity. 2. God—Impartiality.
3. Suffering—Religious aspects—Christianity. I. Howard, Deborah. II. Title.
BT96.3.M33 2008
248.8'6—dc22

                    2008024584

CONTENTS

ACKNOWLEDGMENTS

First, I'd like to extend a word of thanks to Theron and Deborah Howard because, if not for them, this book probably wouldn't have been written. The reason is that, frankly, I hadn't even thought of putting the material into book form. But after hearing me teach this material in a biblical counseling class, Theron and Deborah said, "This material is so good and helpful that it ought to be put into a book and made available to others." I thought it was a great idea and asked Deborah to write it with me. *"It's Not Fair!"* owes its shape and form to her writing skills. She took the material, shaped and honed it, and added some insights. Then I took over, adding some more ideas and altering it here and there. But Deborah did the initial work of getting it ready for publication.

I also want to express my appreciation to Jay Adams for writing a foreword to the book. My thanks also go to John MacArthur, Joel Beeke, Philip Johnson, Conrad Mbewe, James Newheiser, Ronald Kalifungwa, and Joel James for reading the book and writing an endorsement for it. My wife also did her usual thing in proofreading the book and making some suggestions about words or expressions that might improve the way some statement was made. Thanks go to her, my helpmeet and friend for more than fifty years.

My gratitude goes to Marvin Padgett, the kind and gracious editorial director at P&R Publishing. He warmed to the idea of the book immediately and has been an encouragement to us during its development.

And of course, my praise goes to the great and glorious God who is everything and more than this book portrays Him to be.

FOREWORD

All I can say is: "It's not fair!" How is it that Wayne gets to write such a good book and not me? All kidding aside, this is a book you'll want to read, reread, and pass on to someone else. He's right: you do hear those words all the time—not only from counselees, but from family, friends, and (why not admit it?) your own lips as well.

Not only has Wayne written from a biblical perspective, but along the way he has taught essential doctrine about God's sovereignty that alone can help you think rightly about the many matters that trouble you and will keep you from complaining. In addition, following the scriptural patterns he sets forth will keep you from causing yourself (and others) many of the troubles you complain about.

This book, while meaty, is not cooked to the point that it is dry and abstract. It is seasoned by the maturity of the cook's ways with words and garnished by him with useful quotations. There is plenty in it that will help you to keep your daily living for the Lord on course. Indeed, it might even be read in a "quiet hour" along with the Scriptures you are studying. If you examine your life in light of what Wayne says, you may find it helpful as a spiritual purgative as well as a vaccination against a "poor me" attitude. At times, it will probably drive you to prayer.

What more can be said? Get the book—several copies if possible (you'll want to distribute them). Then read, profit, and determine to live more faithfully for our sovereign God, who does all things well!

Jay Adams

INTRODUCTION

For many years as a Christian and as a biblical counselor and teacher, I have recognized that what we know and believe about God is not just a theoretical matter—it has great practical value in terms of how we live life and face its challenges. I know this from the clear teaching of Scripture. I know this from Daniel 11:32: "The people who know their God shall stand firm and take action." I know this from Psalm 46, which describes people who are facing catastrophic circumstances in their environment. The psalm talks about the earth being removed, the mountains being carried into the midst of the seas, the waters roaring and foaming, the mountains trembling and swelling, the nations raging, the kingdoms tottering, and the earth melting.

Wow, what a description of turmoil! These words may describe actual circumstances that have occurred or may occur in the lives of people. They may also symbolically describe horrendous things that happen in our lives on a personal level.

Sometimes such things shake us. Sometimes we lose the things that we think are most solid and stable. Sometimes the things that we value—the things we count on for safety and satisfaction—are ripped away from us.

But whether the events described in Psalm 46 are literal, symbolic, or both, I am sure you would agree that this psalm describes events rightly deserving to be called catastrophic circumstances. In these circumstances, God tells His people what they need to do if they want to respond to these catastrophic circumstances with strength, calmness, and courage: "Be still, and know that I am God" (Ps. 46:10).

In other words, knowing God on a deep level—knowing who and what He is and having a knowledge of His character—will have great *practical* value in terms of handling the denials, refusals, and frightening and painful circumstances that we inevitably face in life. Having a deep personal knowledge of God will help us to handle the events and experiences that come into our lives that we don't desire and sometimes think we don't deserve. This knowledge, when kept on the front burner of our minds and hearts, will keep us from responding to the unpleasant and unwanted experiences in life with the thought and perhaps even the words, "It's not fair."

From years of personal and counseling experience, I know that nothing is more damaging to us spiritually, emotionally, mentally, and behaviorally than responding to the unpleasant, unwanted, and (in our judgment) undeserved circumstances of life with the "it's not fair" attitude. It eats away at us like cancer or leprosy. It is a killer that destroys our joy, hope, faith, love, and usefulness for Christ. And from years of personal and counseling experience coupled with biblical knowledge, I also recognize that nothing is more helpful to us in overcoming the tragic results of being infected with the "it's not fair" attitude than possessing the knowledge of who and what God really is and the implications of that knowledge.

The practical implications of the truths about God presented in this book were recently illustrated by a letter written by Pastor John Sales, reporting on the impact of horrendous and devastating fires that swept through his area of Southern California in October 2007. In that fire thousands of homes were lost, and over five hundred thousand people had to flee from their homes—some of them at a few moments' notice.

In the letter Pastor Sales briefly described the Sunday worship service at his church as the fires were being brought under control. What he wrote bears testimony to the courage and strength that knowing and believing God brings to us. In the midst of what the world would call catastrophe, he and his people were able to avoid the "it's not fair" attitude because of their convictions of the truths presented in this book. His letter, while expressing a note of sorrow, also sounded a note of confidence as the people in the midst of apparent tragedy met to encourage one another and to praise and worship God:

> God truly met us in a wonderful way yesterday! It was so good for our people to be together in worship of God, remembering what really matters in life. It was also very good for our people to hug one another, shed tears, weep with those who weep and rejoice with those who rejoice. It was a great release for people to share

their stories. The church service was packed. One dear 87-year-old Indian matriarch, who lost her home, stood to her feet before the entire congregation and gave testimony to God's grace and urged people to pray that the many on her Indian reservation who do not know Christ would come to know the Savior she loves.

I write this book with the conviction that knowledge of God on the front burner of our minds will be of great value to us in our personal lives and in helping us to fulfill the purpose for which God created and redeemed us—namely, to glorify and enjoy Him forever. In this book I mainly focus on four aspects of the character of God that I think are most useful in counteracting and destroying the devastation that the "it's not fair" attitude causes, and I have also labored to bring out the implications and applications that this knowledge can have in the "now" of life.

Every chapter concludes with some reflection, application, and discussion questions that will assist you to think through the teaching of the chapter and make relevant applications to your own life. Chapter 8 provides two short case studies that demonstrate the ways in which people who know and believe the truths presented in this book respond to the apparent inequities of life as contrasted with those who do not know or believe these truths.

I have also included a list of other books helpful in overcoming an "it's not fair" attitude. My prayer is that God will be pleased to use the contents of this book that way in your own life.

1

The "It's Not Fair" Syndrome

"He doesn't deserve that."

"That's just wrong!"

"This is horrible! It's just not right!"

"What's happening doesn't make any sense. I simply don't understand."

"Someone else is getting the credit that really belongs to me."

"I always get the short end of the stick."

"I didn't do anything wrong, but I'm still being criticized."

No matter what words we use to express this kind of confused disbelief, we're saying the same thing: "It's not fair."

I've been involved in biblical counseling for over forty years. In that length of time, God has allowed me the privilege of helping many people with their problems. Some just wanted to make sure they understood the right (godly) thing to do in a certain situation or relationship. Others had more complex problems that needed more rigorous counseling. And many others had serious issues that required intensive work and prayer to resolve—things such as enslavement to pornography, to drugs or alcohol, or to other forms of immorality. Some counselees were suicidal, others homicidal. Some had long-standing problems of bizarre behavior, depression, or violence. My wife and I have also worked with victims of rape, incest, abandonment, and domestic violence. Nothing surprises me anymore.

There's been a recurring theme throughout my ministry, most commonly expressed as some version of "this is just not fair." It is my hope and prayer that this book will serve those who have asked these questions—whether aloud or to themselves. I think we've all been guilty of this sinful attitude at one time or another. We've heard it over and over. Sometimes we hear it from:

- a person who is angry or depressed about life
- people with physical deformities or limitations
- someone asked to do more than someone else is doing
- someone experiencing hard times when others seem to be gliding happily through life
- someone who is punished for doing something others seem to be getting away with
- those who see everything turn to gold for others while they themselves never seem to catch a break
- the person who gets passed over for promotion even though he thinks he was better qualified
- a person who has just lost a loved one or has just been diagnosed with a serious illness

- the one who gets paid less than someone else for doing the same job
- a single person who remains alone while others find love
- a young woman unable to conceive while others become pregnant without any problem
- a wife whose husband left her for a younger woman after 35 years of marriage
- unhappy parents whose children turned out badly while their friends' kids can do no wrong

"It's not fair" can take many forms, you see. If you listen carefully, you'll hear this statement made by numerous people in the Bible.

- Rachel said it when her sister Leah had children and she didn't.
- The elder brother said it when his father gave the returning prodigal a royal party.
- The Jews said it when they grumbled against God in the wilderness.
- Job said it when he experienced Satan's attacks.
- Jeremiah said it when he was oppressed because of his message of destruction.

Basically, we utter this statement when we believe we are not being treated fairly. Sometimes we are angry at other people, and sometimes we're angry about situations or circumstances. Ultimately, we are angry with God, regardless of how well we disguise it—even to ourselves.

I know a woman who insisted that she was not angry with God but instead felt betrayed and hurt by Him. She tried everything she could to keep from admitting that she was mad at God. We talked about it at length. And there, at the bottom of the exploration into her feelings and attitudes, lay an intense anger toward God, which the young woman confessed and for which she immediately repented. Once this was accomplished, we quickly moved through the circumstances that had brought her to me in the first place. God gave her grace to resolve her "heart problems" and move on to constructive change.

If you are struggling with sinful thoughts, attitudes, and actions, you, like this young woman, will probably find this "it's not fair" syndrome at the root of your problems. Nothing will produce more anger, resentment, bitterness, doubts, bad behavior, divorce, immorality, cruelty, violence, unhappiness, and depression than the idea that you're experiencing something unfair.

What can we do once we recognize that we have a problem in this area? We must counteract this attitude with helpful biblical truth. Nothing will be more useful than revisiting the glorious truths about various aspects of God's character. Once we saturate our minds with these magnificent attributes of our loving Father, we will find that it will not only affect our sinful attitudes, but will also affect the way we handle the consequences of our difficulties.

Sometimes, when our hearts are aching, we may think that what we need is the loving embrace of a compassionate friend. And sure, that helps us feel better. But it's only a temporary sensation. What actually moves us past our self-absorbed sorrow is a generous dose of solid biblical teaching on the following attributes of God:

- His wisdom
- His love
- His sovereignty
- His justice

Some of you may think this book needs to focus more deeply on the pain of suffering. You might be seeking more compassion than these pages provide. And yes, I know how it feels to have my heart broken. My wife and I have experienced hardships and personal losses. So please don't think I'm separated from your personal depth of suffering. No matter how hard you prepare for a crisis, I know how much it hurts to go through it.

"But thinking through the theology of suffering, and resolving in advance how you will respond, however praiseworthy the exercise, cannot prepare you for the shock of suffering itself. It is like jumping into a bitterly cold lake; you can brace yourself for the experience all day, but when you actually jump in the shock to your system will snatch your breath away."[1]

Compassion is critical when we're hurting. But compassion alone will not help us move past the emotions that can cloud our thinking. This book is not intended to be one long, comforting group hug. It's meant to teach and instruct with biblical truths that will help more than fifty good hugs!

"It is through exposure to His Truth that you can find peace in the midst of trouble, hope in the midst of trial and trust in the midst of chaos. If God gives us the grace to knit our will to His, we can find contentment—even in the face of adversity."[2]

For some of you, this book will be a reminder of the truths you've already learned. For others, this may be the first time you've experienced this kind of focused instruction on these vitally important attributes of Almighty God.

"My Times Are in Thy Hand"

My times are in thy hand;
My God, I wish them there;
My life, my friends, my soul, I leave
Entirely to thy care.

My times are in thy hand,
Whatever they may be;
Pleasing or painful, dark or bright,
As best may seem to thee.

My times are in thy hand;
Why should I doubt or fear?
My Father's hand will never cause
His child a needless tear.

My times are in thy hand,
Jesus the Crucified;
Those hands my cruel sins had pierced
Are now my guard and guide.

—*William F. Lloyd, 1824*

REFLECTION, APPLICATION, AND DISCUSSION QUESTIONS

1. Do you agree that the "it's not fair" attitude is a very common one among human beings? Why?

2. What kinds of problems does the "it's not fair" attitude produce? Why are these problems so serious?

3. What are some of the circumstances in which people are prone to respond with an "it's not fair" attitude?

4. What biblical illustrations of people who manifested this attitude were mentioned in this chapter? Describe what was going on in their lives at the time.

5. Can you think of any other people in the Bible who demonstrated this attitude? Describe their circumstances at the time.

6. Do you ever find yourself thinking in terms of "I don't deserve this" or "Why am I being treated this way?" Describe the circumstances in which you have manifested or are manifesting this attitude.

7. What should we do when we recognize that we have a problem in this area? What do we really need in order to overcome this destructive attitude?

2

THE OMNISCIENCE AND WISDOM OF GOD AND THE "IT'S NOT FAIR" SYNDROME

Sometimes, people who feel they aren't being treated fairly have some confusion about how God works in their lives. They may decide that perhaps God doesn't know what's transpiring in their lives or that He doesn't understand the consequences these problems could bring. Others may suffer under the misconception that these things have come to pass as a giant divine mistake. Still others operate under the belief that if God were truly good and were genuinely concerned about us, surely He would somehow do things differently.

How many of us have been guilty of giving God "much-needed advice" instead of seeking Him in heartfelt prayer? But God doesn't need our advice. He desires our trust. We can't impart anything new to Him. He already knows more than we do about . . . well, everything!

Sometimes the things that happen to us in life leave us confused and perplexed. When we arrive at that point, will we still have faith and trust?

Let's examine some biblical passages about God's extraordinary omniscience.

⌐ OMNISCIENCE ⌐
THE WISDOM AND KNOWLEDGE OF GOD

The book of Job contains a record of a man who thought he wasn't being treated fairly. He thought that somehow God was making a big mistake. Job questioned God's wisdom, forgetting that God doesn't make mistakes. He never misjudges anything. He never lacks information. There is nothing God doesn't know about the past, the present, or the future.

In chapters 38 to 40 of the book of Job, God gives Job divine counsel. How did He handle it? Did He tell Job how sorry He was that things had gotten cockeyed? No. Instead, He reminded Job of who He is, of His many attributes—the main one being His omniscience (His limitless wisdom and knowledge).

God's primary argument to Job was this: "Who do you think you are?" He began His counseling session like this:

Then the LORD answered Job out of the whirlwind and said: . . . "Where were you when I laid the foundation of the earth? Tell me, if you have understanding. Who determined its measurements—surely you know! Or who stretched the line upon it? On what were its bases sunk, or who laid its cornerstone, when the morning stars sang together and all the sons of God shouted for joy? Or who shut in the sea with doors when it burst out of the womb, when I made clouds its garment, and thick darkness its swaddling band, and prescribed limits for it and set bars and doors, and said, 'Thus far shall you come, and no farther, and here shall your proud waves be stayed'?" (Job 38:1, 4–11)

The rest of this chapter continues in the same vein.

In reference to the wisdom and knowledge of God, Isaiah 46:9–10 proclaims, "For I am God, and there is no other; I am God, and there is none like me, declaring the end from the beginning and from ancient times things not yet done, saying, 'My counsel shall stand, and I will accomplish all my purpose.'"

In Matthew 6:8, we read, "Do not be like them [pagan Gentiles], for your Father knows what you need before you ask him."

Matthew 10:29–30 says, "Are not two sparrows sold for a penny? And not one of them will fall to the ground apart from your Father. But even the hairs of your head are all numbered."

In Hebrews 4:13, we're told, "And no creature is hidden from his sight, but all are naked and exposed to the eyes of him to whom we must give account."

In one of my favorite passages, Paul expresses his amazement at the scope of God's wisdom: "Oh, the depth of the riches and wisdom and knowledge of God! How unsearchable are his judgments and how inscrutable his ways! 'For who has known the mind of the Lord, or who has been his counselor?' 'Or who has given a gift to him that he might be repaid?' For from him and through him and to him are all things. To him be glory forever. Amen" (Rom. 11:33–36).

You see, God is so wise that He never needs counsel or advice from anyone else. No one has ever plumbed the depths of God's infinite wisdom. The extent of His knowledge is absolutely beyond our comprehension. He possesses all the knowledge that He could ever need and will therefore make right decisions and judgments about every aspect of our existence.

GOD KNOWS EVERYTHING ABOUT US, TOO

The passages quoted above teach us something about God's omniscience. Included in that omniscience is His complete personal knowledge of each of us. Psalm 139 demonstrates this personal perspective of His omniscience as well as His omnipresence. *Omniscience* speaks of God's knowledge of all things. Simply put, His *omnipresence* is His ability to be everywhere at the same time. Psalm 139 speaks volumes about the sovereignty of God, so I will quote some portions of it for you:

> O LORD, you have searched me and known me!
> You know when I sit down and when I rise up;
>   you discern my thoughts from afar.
> You search out my path and my lying down
>   and are acquainted with all my ways.
> Even before a word is on my tongue,
>   behold, O LORD, you know it altogether.

You hem me in, behind and before,
  and lay your hand upon me.
Such knowledge is too wonderful for me;
  it is high; I cannot attain it.

Where shall I go from your Spirit?
  Or where shall I flee from your presence?
If I ascend to heaven, you are there!
  If I make my bed in Sheol [the place for departed
  spirits, the grave], you are there!
If I take the wings of the morning
  and dwell in the uttermost parts of the sea,
even there your hand shall lead me,
  and your right hand shall hold me.
If I say, "Surely the darkness shall cover me,
  and the light about me be night,"
even the darkness is not dark to you;
  the night is bright as the day,
  for darkness is as light with you.

For you formed my inward parts;
  you knitted me together in my mother's womb.
I praise you, for I am fearfully and wonderfully
  made.
Wonderful are your works;
  my soul knows it very well.
My frame was not hidden from you,
when I was being made in secret,
  intricately woven in the depths of the earth.
Your eyes saw my unformed substance;
in your book were written, every one of them,

the days that were formed for me,
 when as yet there were none of them.

How precious to me are your thoughts, O God!
 How vast is the sum of them!
If I would count them, they are more than the sand.
 I awake, and I am still with you. . . .

Search me, O God, and know my heart!
 Try me and know my thoughts!
And see if there be any grievous way in me,
 and lead me in the way everlasting! (Ps. 139:1–18,
 23–24)

What an incredible expression of God's utter knowledge of us—inside and out. His knowledge of us is personal and active. He's not sitting there idly waiting to see what will come about. He is aggressively and directly overseeing our lives and searching our hearts.

Not only does God know us better than we know ourselves, but He knew us before we knew ourselves. Ahead of time, God knows what we're going to think and what we're going to say. He knows it all!

The psalmist clearly understands that God's thoughts are beyond our comprehension. They are so vast and numerous that we couldn't begin to count them—more than the grains of sand on all the shores and in all the seas of the earth! God's wisdom simply cannot be quantified.

He knows everything in the universe, but besides that, He knows everything there is to know about us—our thoughts, our bodies, our dreams, our sins, our motives, and our activities. He knows what and whom we love. He sees right into our very beings. He knows exactly what makes us tick. This is not a God who makes tragic mistakes regarding the direction and design of our lives!

How These Truths Can Overcome the "It's Not Fair" Syndrome

These great truths about God's omniscience, wisdom, and omnipresence have tremendous implications for moving us beyond our "it's not fair" thinking. In fact, I've found that correcting our theology automatically corrects our wrong thinking and doing. *What we believe about God always affects the way we live our lives.*

1. For instance, if we know and believe that God is all-wise and fully aware of everything in our lives, we will not make the same mistake Job made (questioning God's wisdom or goodness). Such knowledge reminds us that God is all-sufficient in the decisions He makes about the way He orders our lives.

The implication of this truth is that we will be better able to embrace whatever He brings us, knowing that all things fall within His good, perfect, and acceptable will for us. We may not understand *why* He does what He does, but we know that what He does is ultimately for our good and for His glory. That should be enough for us.

2. Here is another implication. If we know and believe that God is all-wise and that He really does know what is best for us, for the world, and for the church, then we will be able to stand fast in the face of opposition. We can rejoice in the

Lord always. We will respond to difficulties without becoming hopeless or angry or bitter because we know that God is wise and strong enough to know how to handle tough situations. He is perfectly capable of working all things together for good. No situation is too difficult for God to devise a successful way of handling it. It might be too tough for us to figure it out, but never too tough for Him.

3. Those who know that God is all-wise are able to fully believe this statement in 1 Corinthians 10:13: "No temptation has overtaken you that is not common to man. God is faithful, and he will not let you be tempted beyond your ability, but with the temptation he will also provide the way of escape, that you may be able to endure it." We may not immediately see the way of escape, but we believe God provides one, and this belief keeps us from giving up.

4. If we know and believe that God is all-wise, we will do what Proverbs 3:5–6 commands: "Trust in the LORD with all your heart, and do not lean on your own understanding. In all your ways acknowledge him, and he will make straight your paths." It's His job to direct our paths. It's our job to remain trusting *no matter what!*

5. If we know and believe that God is all-wise, we will be glad to do what James 1:2 says we should do: "Count it all joy, my brothers, when you meet trials of various kinds." We rejoice because of the blessing that comes from our trials.

6. If we know and believe that God is all-wise, we will be convinced that God's interpretation of reality is the only one that is 100 percent accurate. *His Word*, and not *our feelings*, is the standard and definition of reality and truth.

7. If we know and believe that God is all-wise, we will trust that He is doing the right thing even when we don't fully understand why He has allowed certain things to happen.

8. If we know and believe that God is all-wise, we'll realize that God alone knows why we have problems. He knows what causes our human difficulties and why we do what we do. He also knows how they can be resolved.

9. If we know and believe that God is all-wise, we will no longer look to psychologists and psychiatrists for understanding man, his problems, and their earthly solutions. Instead, we will look to God and God alone for our answers. This will involve the careful study of His Word.

10. If we know and believe that God is all-wise, we will desire our thoughts and words to be reflections of His truth; we will love the truth and hate falsehood.

These are only a few of the many ways in which our recognition of the wisdom and omniscience of God can impact our lives. Perhaps we can sum it up by reflecting on the words of my wife's favorite hymn, as we face the conundrums of life.

"God Moves in a Mysterious Way"

God moves in a mysterious way his wonders to perform;
He plants his footsteps in the sea, and rides upon the
storm.
Deep in unfathomable mines of never-failing skill

He treasures up his bright designs, and works his sovereign will.

Ye fearful saints, fresh courage take; the clouds ye so
   much dread
Are big with mercy, and shall break in blessings on
   your head.
Judge not the Lord by feeble sense, but trust him for
   his grace;
Behind a frowning providence he hides a smiling face.

His purposes will ripen fast, unfolding ev'ry hour;
The bud may have a bitter taste, but sweet will be the
   flow'r.
Blind unbelief is sure to err, and scan his work in
   vain;
God is his own interpreter, and he will make it plain.

—William Cowper, 1774

REFLECTION, APPLICATION, AND DISCUSSION QUESTIONS

1. What does God's omniscience really entail? Define the term *omniscience*.

2. What problem was Job really struggling with in reference to God?

3. What was God's primary counsel to Job when He addressed this problem?

4. What are some of the main teachings about God's omniscience in Psalm 139?

5. This chapter mentioned that sometimes we are prone to want to give God advice or counsel.

   a. When and in what circumstances are you most prone to do this?

   b. Can you recall times in the Bible when people have tried to do this with our Lord Jesus Christ?

   c. How did Jesus respond to them?

   d. When have you most recently either done or been tempted to do this?

   e. Why is this a foolish thing to do?

6. What does the fact of God's omniscience have to do with overcoming the "it's not fair" syndrome? How does the "it's not fair" attitude question the wisdom of God?

7. List some of the practical implications for us in our lives of the doctrine of God's infinite wisdom. How can knowing and believing this great truth about God help us in our daily living? What effect should it have on us?

8. Choose three Scripture passages about God's wisdom that mean the most to you, and explain why.

9. Choose two verses from this chapter, and work on memorizing them.

10. Review and meditate on the hymn with which this chapter closed and answer the following questions:

    a. What does this hymn teach us about God and what He is and does?

b. What figures of speech does the poet use to describe God and His ways?

c. What is the poet trying to convey about God through these figures of speech?

d. What does this hymn indicate we should and should not do in reference to God?

e. What, in particular, does this hymn indicate about the wisdom of God?

PS. 103:11

3

THE LOVE OF GOD AND THE "IT'S NOT FAIR" SYNDROME

Living of oneself ~~self~~ for the benifit of others

"LORD, DO YOU NOT CARE?"

Another observation I've been able to make from thousands of hours of counseling sessions is that when people develop the "it's not fair" attitude, you can almost count on the fact that they have lost sight of not only the wisdom of God, but also the vast love of God. Through our work together, the Holy Spirit reminds and convicts them of this important aspect of God's character.

When undergoing severe trial and heartache it's sometimes tempting to question God's love for us. It's tempting but wrong. When we examine the extent of God's love for us, our doubts in that regard should shame us intensely.

We're not the only ones who question God's love for us. Scripture shows us that this was the case in biblical times as well. It was certainly true of the disciples in Mark 4:38. During an intense storm at sea, the disciples despaired of their lives while Jesus peacefully slept in the stern of the boat. They came to Him and asked, "Teacher, do you not care that we are perishing?" The passage goes on to say that Christ awoke and rebuked the storm. Immediately there was a great calm. To His disciples, He said, "Why are you so afraid? Have you still no faith?" (v. 40). They had traveled with Him for some time, at that point. He rebuked their faithlessness in the face of danger.

The lesson is the same for us. Should we despair for our lives, our circumstances, or our loved ones when we know that Christ is in control? Is our confidence in His love for us so flimsy that it leaves us when we're faced with tough times? Are we spiritual wimps?

Martha demonstrated this tendency in Luke 10:38–42. Martha labored busily in the kitchen to prepare and serve a meal for Jesus and His disciples. Her sister, Mary, sat at Jesus' feet, listening to His teaching. So Martha, with her "it's not fair" attitude, came to Jesus and said, "Lord, do you not care that my sister has left me to serve alone? Tell her then to help me" (v. 40). Instead, Jesus rebuked her: "Martha, Martha, you are anxious and troubled about many things, but one thing is necessary. Mary has chosen the good portion, which will not be taken away from her" (vv. 41–42).

Yes, we are commanded to take our responsibilities in life seriously, but we are here shown that, first, our eyes are to remain focused on the Lord. That is our chief responsibility. How many times do we allow the mundane chores and "busyness" of our lives to cloud our vision of Him? *Nothing* should occlude our view of the Lord.

Peter also left us an example that this syndrome was alive and well with even one of Christ's most beloved disciples. John 21 describes Christ's restoring Peter to fellowship with Himself and leadership in ministry to His people. After this restoration, He proceeded to tell Peter in what way he was to die (by crucifixion—according to church history, Peter chose to be crucified upside down, so that he would not be in the same posture as his Lord). Jesus told Peter in verse 18, "Truly, truly, I say to you, when you were young, you used to dress yourself and walk wherever you wanted, but when you are old, you will stretch out your hands, and another will dress you and carry you where you do not want to go."

Just in case we were confused about His meaning, the account parenthetically goes on to explain what Jesus meant: "(This he said to show by what kind of death he was to glorify God.) And after saying this he said to him, 'Follow me'" (v. 19).

Immediately, Peter's response to this revelation was to look at John and ask Christ, "What about this man?" (John 21:21). And Jesus again put Peter in his place: "If it is my will that he remain until I come, what is that to you? You follow me!" (v. 22). Look at Peter's reaction. In light of what Jesus had just told him, Peter wanted to know how John would die. And Jesus basically told him, "That's none of your business, Peter. *You follow Me!*"

The lesson to us is equally clear. When faced with even the hardest things, our duty is to follow Him. We are to keep our eyes on our precious Lord. We are to trust and not falter.

Yes, the disciples faltered from time to time. But so do those of us who develop the "it's not fair" attitude. Perhaps it would be good for us to examine our own thoughts about God's love for us.

"AMAZING LOVE, HOW CAN IT BE?"

Let's take a look at some of the Bible's teaching regarding the love of God for His children. That's where we need to go to counteract the effects of the "it's not fair!" syndrome. By the way, what do I mean when I use the term *syndrome*? In this context I mean it as a set of characteristics identifying a certain attitude or attitudes.

God's love is described throughout the Old and New Testaments. These verses are just a few to consider when you need a reminder of His love.

unchanging

"For as high as the heavens are above the earth, so great is his steadfast love toward those who fear him" (Ps. 103:11).

"Give thanks to the LORD, for he is good, for his steadfast love endures forever" (Ps. 136:1).

"The LORD is gracious and merciful, slow to anger and abounding in steadfast love" (Ps. 145:8).

"Who shall separate us from the love of Christ? Shall tribulation, or distress, or persecution, or famine, or nakedness, or danger, or sword? . . . No, in all these things we are more than conquerors through him who loved us. For I am sure that neither death nor life, nor angels nor rulers, nor things present nor things to come, nor powers, nor height nor depth, nor anything else in all creation, will be able to separate us from the love of God in Christ Jesus our Lord" (Rom. 8:35, 37–39). Even our own sinful attitudes will not separate us from God's love. He loves us just as much when we fail as He does when we're faithful. His love is lavished on us without conditions.

"I have been crucified with Christ. It is no longer I who live, but Christ who lives in me. And the life I now live in the flesh I live by faith in the Son of God, who loved me and gave himself for me" (Gal. 2:20). Many Christians overlook this point. When Christ gave Himself for us, He bought us. He owns us. He could have ended our lives at the moment of our spiritual regeneration, but He didn't. Instead, He left us here as His representatives on earth.

Since we are owned by Christ, therefore, we are His slaves. And a slave, by his very nature, must live to please his master. Our whole existence as slaves should be directed toward serving Him. If our lives are all about *self*-fulfillment, we will experience unsteadiness. But if our goal is pleasing Christ, we will begin to see our lives in relation to Him. That brings steadiness to our lives. We are to live to please our Master. Since He owns us, we *must* obey His commands, you see, because we are dependent on Him for everything! In our deceitful pride, we live as if it's all about us. Actually, it's all about Him.

"But God, being rich in mercy, because of the great love with which he loved us, even when we were dead in our trespasses, made us alive together with Christ" (Eph. 2:4–5a). Did you catch that? Even before we loved Him, while we were still dead in our trespasses, He loved us. He didn't wait until we *deserved* His love. And thank God for that—otherwise, He would never love us. We could never do anything to merit His love. It is freely given to His children.

"And walk in love, as Christ loved us and gave himself up for us, a fragrant offering and sacrifice to God" (Eph. 5:2).

"Humble yourselves, therefore, under the mighty hand of God so that at the proper time he may exalt you, casting all your anxieties on him, because he cares for you" (1 Peter 5:6–7).

"Anyone who does not love does not know God, because God is love" (1 John 4:8). This does not merely state that God loves. It says that God *is* love. Love is a part of His very nature. In fact, it is impossible for God not to love where His children are concerned because He is absolutely holy. It is impossible for Him to be anything but perfectly good.

"In this is love, not that we have loved God but that he loved us and sent his Son to be the propitiation [payment] for our sins" (1 John 4:10).

I hope these passages have shown you that God's love is a *fact.* Now let's explore some of the manifestations of this great love.

HOW DOES GOD'S LOVE MANIFEST ITSELF IN OUR LIVES?

The most crucial way in which God's love shows up in our lives is the way in which God brought us to salvation through faith in His Son, Jesus Christ. All other manifestations pale in comparison with this one.

In salvation, He imparted life to us, though we were dead in trespasses and sins:

- by raising us up with Christ, in giving us grace to handle the trials of life
- by comforting us in our afflictions
- by giving us hope for the present and the future
- by making peace and joy available to us in the midst of trials and helping us to overcome the controlling influence of the lusts of the flesh
- by giving us meaning and purpose for living
- by making it possible for us to have lives that are characterized by the fruit of the Spirit
- by giving us the right to sit with Christ in heavenly places

"The cross, then, is the place where God's justice and love meet. God retains the integrity of his justice; God pours out the fullness of his love. . . . The death of God's own Son is the only adequate gauge of what God thinks of my sin; the death of God's own Son is the only basis on which I may be forgiven that sin. The cross is the triumph of justice and love."[1]

Giving His Son on our behalf was the greatest sacrifice that God could ever make. He did this to provide a way across the chasm of sin and eternal punishment. And that way is found only in Jesus, who taught us, "I am the way, and the truth, and the life. No one comes to the Father except through me" (John 14:6).

"For God so loved the world, that he gave his only Son, that whoever believes in him should not perish but have eternal life" (John 3:16).

"He who did not spare his own Son but gave him up for us all, how will he not also with him graciously give us all things?" (Rom. 8:32).

God's love is especially manifested in His willingness to freely forgive sinners—deserving hell and wrath—when they repent and believe in Christ. In the preceding section, we saw that God gave His precious Son on our behalf. The other half of that great act is that in doing so, He forgave all the sins of His people.

"Blessed is the one whose transgression is forgiven, whose sin is covered. Blessed is the man against whom the LORD counts no iniquity, and in whose spirit there is no deceit" (Ps. 32:1–2).

"Behold, it was for my welfare that I had great bitterness: but in love you have delivered my life from the pit of destruction, for you have cast all my sins behind your back" (Isa. 38:17).

"Seek the LORD while he may be found; call upon him while he is near; let the wicked forsake his way, and the unrighteous man his thoughts; let him return to the LORD, that he may have compassion on him, and to our God, for he will abundantly pardon" (Isa. 55:6–7).

"In him we have redemption through his blood, the forgiveness of our trespasses, according to the riches of his grace, which he lavished upon us, in all wisdom and insight" (Eph. 1:7–8).

God's love provides hope for His children and equips us to increasingly overcome iniquity. We will not attain sinlessness on this side of heaven, but we are to aspire to this perfect standard. We are to make every effort to be holy as God is holy.

"If the Spirit of him who raised Jesus from the dead dwells in you, he who raised Christ Jesus from the dead will also give life to your mortal bodies through his Spirit who dwells in you" (Rom. 8:11). We are not enslaved to our passions and desires any longer. God has put those old things to death and causes us, through the Holy Spirit, to conform to His desires, not our own.

"For sin will have no dominion over you, since you are not under law but under grace" (Rom. 6:14). When we become believers in Christ, we have a new Master. We are no longer under sin's rulership of our lives.

"Therefore, if anyone is in Christ, he is a new creation. The old has passed away; behold, the new has come" (2 Cor. 5:17).

"But I say, walk by the Spirit, and you will not gratify the desires of the flesh" (Gal. 5:16).

"But that is not the way you learned Christ!—assuming that you have heard about him and were taught in him, as the truth is in Jesus, to put off your old self, which belongs to your former manner of life and is corrupt through deceitful desires, and to be renewed in the spirit of your minds, and to put on the new self, created after the likeness of God in true righteousness and holiness" (Eph. 4:20–24).

"His divine power has granted to us all things that pertain to life and godliness, through the knowledge of him who called us to his own glory and excellence" (2 Peter 1:3). We have everything we need to live wise and obedient lives—lives pleasing to the Lord. If that were not possible, He wouldn't have commanded it.

The love of God makes itself known in that He willingly adopts us into His family as full-fledged children and grants us all the privileges of that adoption. We are not like guests in heaven, nor are we merely like tourists or honored visitors. We are considered legitimate heirs of the kingdom, co-heirs with Christ.

"For you did not receive the spirit of slavery to fall back into fear, but you have received the Spirit of adoption as sons, by whom we cry, 'Abba! Father!' The Spirit himself bears witness with our spirit that we are children of God, and if children, then heirs—heirs of God and fellow heirs with Christ, provided we suffer with him in order that we may also be glorified with him" (Rom. 8:15–17).

"And because you are sons, God has sent the Spirit of his Son into our hearts, crying, 'Abba! Father!' So you are no longer a slave, but a son, and if a son, then an heir through God" (Gal. 4:6).

"In love he predestined us for adoption through Jesus Christ, according to the purpose of his will, to the praise of his glorious grace, with which he has blessed us in the Beloved" (Eph. 1:4b–6).

"Blessed be the God and Father of our Lord Jesus Christ! According to his great mercy, he has caused us to be born again to a living hope through the resurrection of Jesus Christ from the dead, to an inheritance that is imperishable, undefiled, and unfading, kept in heaven for you, who by God's power are being guarded through faith for a salvation ready to be revealed in the last time" (1 Peter 1:3–5).

"See what kind of love the Father has given to us, that we should be called children of God; and so we are" (1 John 3:1a).

Another manifestation of God's love to us is that whenever we are afflicted, even by His own hand, He shares that affliction. He can do this because of the afflictions He experienced on our behalf. Just as we share in His suffering, He shares in ours.

"Then the LORD said, 'I have surely seen the affliction of my people who are in Egypt and have heard their cry because of their taskmasters. I know their sufferings.'" (Ex. 3:7).

"In all their [His people's] affliction he was afflicted, and the angel of his presence saved them; in his love and in his pity he redeemed them; he lifted them up and carried them all the days of old" (Isa. 63:9).

"When he saw the crowds, he had compassion for them, because they were harassed and helpless, like sheep without a shepherd" (Matt. 9:36).

"When Jesus saw her weeping, and the Jews who had come with her also weeping, he was deeply moved in his spirit and greatly troubled. And he said, 'Where have you laid him?' They said to him, 'Lord, come and see.' Jesus wept" (John 11:33–35). Our Lord does not remain untouched in the face of our heartache. He is moved by compassion to share our sorrow.

"For we do not have a high priest [Christ] who is unable to sympathize with our weaknesses, but one who in every respect has been tempted as we are, yet without sin" (Heb. 4:15).

God's love is made manifest in our lives in that He never forgets or abandons His people. Even during our darkest times, He is with us—even if, in our forgetful hearts, He seems far away. We may forget Him, but He never forgets us. It reminds me of an old saying, "If you feel that God is far away, guess who moved." One thing is for sure: He didn't!

"Fear not, for I have redeemed you; I have called you by name, you are mine. When you pass through the waters, I will be with you; and through the rivers, they shall not overwhelm you; when you walk through fire you shall not be burned, and the flame shall not consume you. . . . You are precious in my eyes, and honored, and I love you" (Isa. 43:1b–2, 4a). He is right beside us through every trial.

"Can a woman forget her nursing child, that she should have no compassion on the son of her womb? Even these may forget, yet I will not forget you. Behold, I have engraved you on the palms of my hands; your walls are continually before me" (Isa. 49:15–16). Here God calls attention to what is considered to be one of the closest and tightest of all human relationships—that of a mother's love for her child. The point of this passage is that even a mother's love may fail, but God's love is exceedingly more dependable. Our relationship with Him is the one relationship that cannot and will not be broken.

" 'For the mountains may depart and the hills be removed, but my steadfast love shall not depart from you, and my covenant of peace shall not be removed,' says the Lord, who has compassion on you" (Isa. 54:10).

"And behold, I am with you always, to the end of the age" (Matt. 28:20b).

"I will not leave you as orphans; I will come to you" (John 14:18).

"I will never leave you nor forsake you" (Heb. 13:5b, quoting Josh. 1:5). How comforting are the promises of God!

God's love is made manifest when He chastens and disciplines us. He uses suffering to mold us into who and what He wants us to be. No, it doesn't feel good at the time, but we should thank Him that He does it. It gives us evidence that He loves us (or He wouldn't do it) and that we are being made perfect by these trials.

Out of this chastening comes the peaceable fruit of righteousness. Through these difficulties we become more like Christ and will enjoy more of His grace and help. When we pass through these trials, we are humbled and made submissive to His will and thereby fall into a deeper fellowship with

Him as we increasingly come to rely on Him. These difficulties loosen the hold of the world on us, and we develop greater longings for our heavenly home.

"For I consider that the sufferings of this present time are not worth comparing with the glory that is to be revealed to us" (Rom. 8:18).

"Indeed, we felt that we had received the sentence of death. But that was to make us rely not on ourselves but on God who raises the dead" (2 Cor. 1:9).

"So we do not lose heart. Though our outer nature is wasting away, our inner nature is being renewed day by day. For this slight momentary affliction is preparing for us an eternal weight of glory beyond all comparison" (2 Cor. 4:16–17).

"So to keep me from being too elated by the surpassing greatness of the revelations, a thorn was given me in the flesh, a messenger of Satan to harass me, to keep me from being too elated. Three times I pleaded with the Lord about this, that it should leave me. But he said to me, 'My grace is sufficient for you, for my power is made perfect in weakness.' Therefore I will boast all the more gladly of my weaknesses, so that the power of Christ may rest upon me. For the sake of Christ, then, I am content with weaknesses, insults, hardships, persecutions, and calamities. For when I am weak, then I am strong" (2 Cor. 12:7–10).

" 'My son, do not regard lightly the discipline of the Lord, nor be weary when reproved by him. For the Lord disciplines the one he loves, and chastises every son whom he receives.' It is for discipline that you have to endure. God is treating you as sons. For what son is there whom his father does not discipline? If you are left without discipline, in which all have participated, then you are illegitimate children and not sons. . . . For the moment all discipline seems painful rather than pleasant, but later it yields the peaceful fruit of righteousness to those who have been trained by it" (Heb. 12:5b–8, 11, quoting Prov. 3:11–12).

"Beloved, do not be surprised at the fiery trial when it comes upon you to test you, as though something strange were happening to you. But rejoice insofar as you share Christ's sufferings, that you may also rejoice and be glad when his glory is revealed" (1 Peter 4:12–13).

"Those whom I love, I reprove and discipline" (Rev. 3:19a).

> Amazing love!
> How can it be
> That Thou my Lord
> Shouldst die for me?[2]

IMPLICATIONS OF THE LOVE OF GOD FOR OUR DAILY LIVES

What are the implications of this deep and faithful love that God shows to His children? Let's take a look at a few:

- Since love, mercy, and grace are aspects of God's nature, He cannot act in an unloving way toward His children.
- Since love, mercy, and grace are parts of God's nature, He will never cease to be loving, gracious, and merciful to His children.

- Since God is loving, gracious, and merciful, He (not any of us) is the standard when defining real love.
- Since the Bible declares God to be of infinite holiness, wisdom, and love, we must choose to believe that the difficulties we experience are designed to achieve positive benefits in our lives and in the world around us. We must choose to walk by faith rather than sight. What exactly does that mean? It means that we must choose to view God and His purposes through the lens of Scripture rather than by our own feelings or opinions. It means that we will stop thinking of God as unfair.

When we see our circumstances through a spiritual lens, it forces us to remove ourselves from the equation. What is more important—having everything go our way, or trusting God to order our circumstances *His way* for our best good and for His glory?

It reminds me of the passage where Jesus foretells His death: "From that time Jesus began to show his disciples that he must go to Jerusalem and suffer many things from the elders and chief priests and scribes, and be killed, and on the third day be raised. And Peter took him aside and began to rebuke him, saying, 'Far be it from you, Lord! This shall never happen to you.' But he turned and said to Peter, 'Get behind me, Satan!'" (Matt. 16:21–23a).

Peter could not imagine our Lord's death in such a way. Out of his passion and love for Christ, he took it upon himself to rebuke Him. In his own way, Peter was acting on this attitude: "No, that couldn't be. It just wouldn't be right. I won't have it!" And for that, the Lord calls him "Satan."

Wow! That might seem like harsh language coming from our Lord, but note what He says next, almost as a word of explanation. Continuing in verse 23, we read, "You are a hindrance to me. For you are not setting your mind on the things of God, but on the things of man."

There it is—and from the Lord Jesus Christ Himself! When we want to give God advice and complain and whine against His divine plans for us or others, we are a *hindrance* to Him. And it's true, when we are more concerned about orchestrating happy lives for ourselves than we are about the fulfillment of God's will—whatever that will is—we're more concerned about the things of man than about the things of God.

Do you want to be a hindrance? Do you want to stand as an obstacle between God and His divine will? Watch out. That's a dangerous place to stand. He *will* overcome.

How, then, can we conform our will to His? How can we stop viewing our lives only from our selfish points of view and instead see the situations in our lives through that spiritual lens?

One thing we can do is to meditate on the love of God as it was and is displayed in Jesus Christ and the sacrifice He made on the cross. That's where the ultimate, irrefutable, undeniable, objective proof of His love can be seen most clearly. When we spend precious time pouting, thinking God doesn't love us, we should measure that love by a lonely hillside outside Jerusalem. Shame on us.

I heartily concur with Jerry Bridges, who writes:

> When we begin to question the love of God, we need to remember who we are. We have absolutely no

claim on His love. We don't deserve one bit of God's goodness to us. . . . I know of nothing that will so quickly cut the nerve of a petulant, "Why did this happen to me?" attitude as a realization of who we are before God, considered in ourselves apart from Christ.

We see then that God loved us when we were totally unworthy, when there was nothing whatsoever within us that would call forth His love.

Any time that we are tempted to doubt God's love for us, we should go back to the Cross. We should reason somewhat in this fashion: If God loved me enough to give His Son to die for me when I was His enemy, surely He loves me enough to care for me now that I am His child. Having loved me to the ultimate extent at the Cross, He cannot possibly fail to love me in my times of adversity. Having given such a priceless gift as His Son, surely He will also give all else that is consistent with His glory and my good.

Note that I said, we should reason. If we are to trust God in adversity, we must use our minds in those times to reason through the great truths of God's sovereignty, wisdom, and love as they are revealed to us in the Scriptures. We must not allow our emotions to hold sway over our minds. Rather, we must seek to let the truth of God rule our minds. Our emotions must become subservient to the truth. This does not mean we do not feel the pain of adversity and heartache. We feel it keenly. Nor does it mean we should seek to bury our emotional pain in a stoic-like attitude. We are meant to feel the pain of adversity, but we must resist allowing that pain to cause us to lapse into hard thoughts about God. . . .

If God's love was sufficient for my greatest need, my eternal salvation, surely it is sufficient for my lesser needs, the adversities I encounter in this life.[3]

Another thing we can do is meditate on the Scriptures that tell us about our Lord's compassion and sympathy for hurting, afflicted people. Here are just a few:

"In all their affliction he was afflicted, and the angel of his presence saved them; in his love and in his pity he redeemed them; he lifted them up and carried them all the days of old" (Isa. 63:9).

"For because he himself has suffered when tempted, he is able to help those who are being tempted" (Heb. 2:18).

What else can we do? We must pause to remind ourselves of the fact that God has promised that He will never abandon us, but that He will be right there with us as we go through our trials.

"Fear not, for I am with you; be not dismayed, for I am your God; I will strengthen you, I will help you, I will uphold you with my righteous right hand" (Isa. 41:10).

"And behold, I am with you always" (Matt. 28:20b).

We must challenge ourselves to continually focus on the blessings that God has given us—especially the ones since we became believers in Christ. Think about the meaning and truth of Ephesians 1:3 ("Blessed be the God and Father of our Lord Jesus Christ, who has blessed us in Christ with every spiritual blessing in the heavenly places.") and strive to follow through in doing what Philippians 4:8 directs ("Finally, brothers, whatever is true, whatever is honorable, whatever is just, whatever is pure, whatever is lovely, whatever is commendable, if there is any excellence, if there is anything worthy of praise, think about these things.").

Another helpful suggestion for refocusing our view from our own to God's is to consider the positive things that our wise, holy, and loving God may want to accomplish through the adversities we experience. Unless we spend time pondering these events, we may miss valuable opportunities to glorify Him through our troubles. Prayerfully ask Him to open our eyes to His truth.

There are so many other ways that God's love directly impacts our lives. I know I've inundated you with biblical passages in this chapter. I did it to illustrate these crucial truths about the love of God. In doing so, I pray that instead of finding them tedious and easily skipped over, you will read them and meditate on them, burdened by the preponderance of biblical evidence that supports this marvelous and humbling aspect of God's character.

If we are still experiencing the "it's not fair" syndrome, it might be helpful to meditate on the words of Samuel Trevor Francis's great hymn, "O The Deep, Deep Love of Jesus!"

"O the Deep, Deep Love of Jesus!"

O the deep, deep love of Jesus!
Vast, unmeasured, boundless, free;
Rolling as a mighty ocean
In its fullness over me.
Underneath me, all around me,
Is the current of thy love;
Leading onward, leading homeward,
To thy glorious rest above.

O the deep, deep love of Jesus!
Spread his praise from shore to shore;
How he loveth, ever loveth,
Changeth never, nevermore;
How he watches o'er his loved ones,
Died to call them all his own;
How for them he intercedeth,
Watcheth o'er them from the throne.

O the deep, deep love of Jesus!
Love of ev'ry love the best:
'Tis an ocean vast of blessing,
'Tis a haven sweet of rest.
O the deep, deep love of Jesus!
'Tis a heav'n of heav'ns to me;
And it lifts me up to glory,
For it lifts me up to thee.

—*Samuel Trevor Francis, 1875*

1. This chapter begins by asserting that people who develop the "it's not fair" attitude have forgotten about not only the wisdom of God but also the love of God. Do you agree with that statement? If so, why? How would forgetting about the immense love of God foster an "it's not fair" attitude?

2. What biblical statements establishing the fact of God's love were given in this chapter?

3. Can you think of any other biblical examples of people who forgot about or questioned God's love?

4. What are the ways that God demonstrates His love toward His children? Be specific.

5. Have there been times in your life when you have forgotten, questioned, or not been encouraged by the reality of God's love for you?

   a. When were those times? What was going on?

   b. What were you thinking about at those times?

   c. What was the result of either forgetting about or questioning the love of God in your life?

   d. What do you think Jude is talking about when he directs his readers to "keep yourselves in the love of God" (v. 21)? Compare this statement with John 15:9–10; 1 John 2:5; Jude 1.

   e. Why is it so important to keep ourselves in the love of God?

f. Why do we lose the sense of His love?

g. How do we keep ourselves in the love of God?

6. Besides the greatest manifestation of God's love in sending His Son into this world and giving Him up as the sacrifice for our sins, what is the most meaningful expression or proof of His love to you?

7. How does seeing our circumstances through the lens of God's love cause us to remove ourselves (our thoughts, feelings, opinions, and desires) from the equation and to trust God to order our circumstances His way?

8. In times of difficulty, what must we do to stop viewing our lives only from our selfish perspective and to start viewing our lives and circumstances from God's point of view, renewing in us the sense and conviction that whatever is going on is within the circumference of God's love for us?

9. What does the hymn "O the Deep, Deep Love of Jesus!" tell us about His love?

a. How does this hymn describe the love of Jesus? Note the specific details of the love of Jesus expressed in this hymn.

b. What figures of speech does this hymn use to describe the love of Jesus?

c. How do these figures of speech relate to the love of Jesus?

d. What does the love of Jesus cause Him to do for us?

e. How should we respond to the love of Jesus? What should it motivate us to do?

God always acts in accordance of what is right. He is the final standard of what is right. His Moral Standard is right

Memory Verse: PS. 145:17

4

RIGHTEOUSNOUS
THE JUSTICE OF GOD AND THE "IT'S NOT FAIR" SYNDROME

WHAT DID I DO TO DESERVE THIS?

I f God is so good, how can He allow things that cause such grief and pain to happen to us? We've already seen that He is omniscient. We've studied the love of God—the reality and truth of it, the manifestations of it, and the implications of it. So if the problem doesn't lie in His wisdom or love for us, then it must be His sense of justice. Right? Let's take a look at the Bible to see what it says about this important characteristic of God.

If you read the book of Job, you'll see that Job wondered about God's justice. In fact, he repeatedly accused God of injustice. The gist of his argument was something like this: "God, I know You are all-powerful and all-knowing. I know that You created the world and everything in it. I know that You give and You take away. I get that. What I don't get is this—where is Your justice? I didn't do anything to deserve what You're giving me right now. I am completely blameless and have spent my whole life honoring You. So what I don't understand is what You think I've done that You have dealt so wrongly with me. Give me a moment of Your attention so I can straighten You out on this issue."

In other words—"it's not fair!"

We see this same confused struggle in Psalm 73. Here we can clearly see that the psalmist has adopted the "it's not fair" mind-set and that it threatens to destroy him. He sees the wicked seemingly prosper while he himself suffers failure even though he tries to live righteously. In verses 12–14, he wrote, "Behold, these are the wicked; always at ease, they increase in riches. All in vain have I kept my heart clean and washed my hands in innocence. For all the day long I have been stricken and rebuked every morning."

In other words—"it's not fair!"

I once counseled a young man who had been abused by a number of people as he was growing up. He'd been abused by his mother and father and by some men who had actually raped him. As a result of this treatment, he confessed that he struggled with big anger and anxiety problems. During the course of my investigation of the data, he said, "I can't figure out why this has happened to me. Why couldn't I have been raised in a happy family like others? I don't know what I've done to deserve all this. Why did God allow these things to happen to me?"

In other words—"it's not fair!"

The problem with which this young man struggled is the same one experienced by Job and by the psalmist, and by many of the people who come to me for counseling—as well as a great many others who do not. The problem may manifest itself through anger or anxiety. It may show up in the form of resentment, bitterness, or discouragement. Many sufferers become doubtful and unstable in their Christian walk.

When we begin to question the fairness or justice of our life circumstances, we can count on the fact that we will also experience many other unpleasant consequences. What we need at a time like this is not someone saying to us, "Aw, poor thing. I don't blame you for being mad at God! I would be, too." What we need is a double dose of teaching on the justice of God. We need to remind ourselves what God says to us in the Bible about His justice and goodness.

BIBLICAL EXAMPLES OF THE PERFECT JUSTICE OF GOD

"Shall not the Judge of all the earth do what is just?" (Gen. 18:25b).

"For the LORD your God is God of gods and Lord of lords, the great, the mighty, and the awesome God, who is not partial and takes no bribe" (Deut. 10:17).

"Therefore, hear me, you men of understanding: far be it from God that he should do wickedness, and from the Almighty that he should do wrong. . . . Of a truth, God will not do wickedly, and the Almighty will not pervert justice" (Job 34:10, 12).

"For you have maintained my just cause; you have sat on the throne, giving righteous judgment" (Ps. 9:4).

"But the LORD sits enthroned forever; he has established his throne for justice, and he judges the world with righteousness; he judges the peoples with uprightness" (Ps. 9:7–8).

"For the LORD is righteous; he loves righteous deeds; the upright shall behold his face" (Ps. 11:7).

 "The LORD is righteous in all his ways and kind in all his works" (Ps. 145:17).

"It was to show his righteousness at the present time, so that he might be just and the justifier of the one who has faith in Jesus" (Rom. 3:26).

"If we confess our sins, he is faithful and just to forgive us our sins and to cleanse us from all unrighteousness" (1 John 1:9).

Righteousness and justice are part of God's holy nature. He *cannot* do anything wrong because to do so would be to violate His very nature. Righteousness is not simply something God *does*—it is part of who He *is!*

This means, of course, that when we accuse God of being unjust, we are flat-out contradicting the clear teaching of the Bible. In fact, we must understand that if we continue to do this, we are really saying that we don't believe the Bible.

I trust that I have established the fact that the Bible declares God to be just and nothing but just in all He does. This means that if we truly belong to Christ, we must exercise faith in what the Bible says even though we may not understand how it is so.

We may start out on our Christian journey thinking, "God needs me." It doesn't take long before we fall to our knees in the recognition that it is we who need Him. We cry out to Him for blessings. But only through our sorrows and suffering can we truly come to the realization that *He* is the greatest blessing of all.

Everything we have is part of God's jurisdiction. It is within His right to take away *all* our comforts, save one—Himself. He'll never take that away from us. And remember, He never takes anything that He didn't give in the first place.

The bottom line is that even if we lost it all, we would still have our relationship with God. That's why this irrevocable relationship should be more important to us than anything else in the world. The other things and people we treasure most must be held up to Him with an open hand and a heart that trusts in His mercy, love, goodness, *and* justice.

We must come to acknowledge that our understanding of justice is finite, whereas God's is infinite. The standard for justice does not reside in our feeble brain cells, but rests instead in the glorious mind of God. It is not His job to conform His thinking to ours. It is our job to conform our thinking to His.

Many factors come into play when we view circumstances from our own earthly viewpoint, with our fleshly, sinful thinking. For one thing, we need to be reminded that all that glitters is not gold, and we cannot judge a book by its cover. Clichés, perhaps, but true nevertheless.

For instance, the writer of Psalm 73 saw the wicked prospering. That perception caused him to openly question God's justice. He spiraled into depression, bitterness, and resentment.

But the psalm doesn't end there. It goes on to say, "Truly you set them [the wicked] in slippery places; you make them fall to ruin" (v. 18). The psalmist came to see that the best the wicked were ever going to have was right now. For these *apparently* prosperous people, the worst was yet to come, whereas the psalmist acknowledges that "when my soul was embittered, when I was pricked in heart, I was brutish and ignorant; I was like a beast toward you. Nevertheless, I am continually with you; you hold my right hand. You guide me with your counsel, and afterward you will receive me to glory" (vv. 21–24). For believers, the best is yet to come!

Note who holds whom in this passage. He holds on to us. If our position depended on our holding on to Him, we'd be helplessly lost. But recognizing that it is God who does the holding should give us great confidence that He will bring us home in the end. We simply cannot fall.

Sometimes the injustice of a situation may be only perceived and not real. On the surface, circumstances may appear a certain way, but behind the scenes is a very different story.

For example, we've probably all had the experience of holding a beautiful, delicious-looking piece of fruit in our hands, only to find a worm or rotten place when we cut or bite into it.

What about this illustration? When walking into the surf on a beautiful sunny day on the beach, everything may look peaceful and calm—that is, until you see a big, black dorsal fin slicing quickly through the water toward you.

We need to understand that the picture is larger than it seems. More is happening than meets the eye in most cases. We can be so easily misinformed, misled, and misguided when we trust our own perceptions of reality. We are not omniscient, remember? Only God is. We can't see beneath the surface. He can. He sees the big picture!

Surely we've known people who are gracious and cheerful on the surface, only to find wickedness and vile contempt underneath their facade. Certainly we've marveled at the prosperity and picture-book happiness of some, only to find out in the end that their lives were rampant with all sorts of sin, depravity, and heartbreak. What about the concept of the tears of a clown? He's smiling and happy on the outside, but inside he's crying tears of sorrow. In many cases, people project just the image they want us to see.

I'm sure we've all heard stories about murderers who commit horrible crimes. In most cases, we hear testimonials to this effect from those who knew them : "He was such a nice, quiet man. He'd do anything for anybody. He was such a great guy. I just can't believe he's done this terrible thing."

The point is this: we can't see beneath the surface—the surface of fruit or water or people. We are exposed to situations that we find seemingly unjust to our earthly vision. The truth of the matter is that we can't see beneath the surface of the events and circumstances of our lives.

Todd Murray, worship pastor at the Bible Church of Little Rock, says that most of the time we desire lives in which we don't need to employ our faith at all! His point is that if we could order our lives in any way we saw fit, we'd make sure that they would be lives of happiness and bliss. They wouldn't include the difficulties and the sorrows.

In other words, we'd never choose to walk through the hard places where we must actually exercise our faith—the troubling times when we experience the greatest growth through adversity. When we're brought to a place where we are forced to utilize our faith in Christ, that's also when we experience the sweetest fellowship with our Lord—the One who never leaves us or forsakes us, who will bear us under the protection of His sheltering wings, who cares about our sorrows so much that He is grieved when we are.

How good our Lord is to us. How faithful and gracious He is to give us what we *need* instead of what we *want*. Yes, it's always a beneficial exercise to review the glorious attributes of God.

Imagine our lives as a giant tapestry. From our vantage point, underneath the tapestry, we see only disjointed colors and knots and loose threads. It doesn't make a lot of sense to us. Sometimes we can dimly make out a pattern, but not clearly. If we could see from God's vantage point, though, we could see all things clearly. From our new vantage point, it would all make sense. The top of the beautiful tapestry displays striking patterns of color that would take our breath away. The intricacies of its design would boggle our senses.

Do we demand to see the finished product now? Can we stand, as the mouse before the plow, with our tiny fists upraised and command God to explain Himself? Do we have the right to insist that He show us all His plans today?

"But who are you, O man, to answer back to God? Will what is molded say to its molder, 'Why have you made me like this?'" (Rom. 9:20). Shame on us! Where is our faith? our trust? our respect and awe for God?

"I would never do that," you might say. But isn't that what we do when we pout and whine and complain about our lot in life? When we do this, we are, in fact, murmuring against Him. We dare not do that! Instead, we must renew our sinful minds with the truth of His Word. Think about it!

What if we're being abused or mistreated by others? If we're innocent of any wrongdoing, don't we have a right to be angry? Isn't it natural to want to get even?

Perhaps it's what comes naturally, but then, as believers, we're not called to act according to our "natural" inclinations. We're called to a higher standard. It is not our job to get even with those who cause us pain and grief. The Bible teaches us that it's God's job to do that—and to do it with absolute justice.

God's justice is our standard. And He tells us in Romans:

> Bless those who persecute you; bless and do not curse them. . . . Repay no one evil for evil, but give thought to do what is honorable in the sight of all. If possible, so far as it depends on you, live peaceably with all. Beloved, never avenge yourselves, but leave it to the wrath of God, for it is written, "Vengeance is mine, I will repay, says the Lord." To the contrary, if your enemy is hungry, feed him; if he is thirsty, give him something to drink; for by so doing you will heap burning coals on his head. Do not be overcome by evil, but overcome evil with good. (Rom. 12:14, 17–21, quoting Deut. 32:35)

That's a far cry from doing what comes naturally, isn't it? But we're told that God's justice repays affliction to those who are afflicting us. And we're reassured that what God begins, He will bring to completion.

"For he will complete what he appoints for me, and many such things are in his mind" (Job 23:14).

"But I trust in you, O LORD; I say, 'You are my God.' My times are in your hand; rescue me from the hand of my enemies and from my persecutors!" (Ps. 31:14–15).

"This is evidence of the righteous judgment of God, that you may be considered worthy of the kingdom of God, for which you are also suffering—since indeed God considers it just to repay with affliction those who afflict you, and to grant relief to you who are afflicted as well as to us, when the Lord Jesus is revealed from heaven with his mighty angels in flaming fire" (2 Thess. 1:5–8a).

"For the eyes of the Lord are on the righteous, and his ears are open to their prayer. But the face of the Lord is against those who do evil" (1 Peter 3:12, quoting Ps. 34:15–16a).

Now, does God do this on *our* timetable or His own? We are to trust Him in all things—including *when* He chooses to act. It is enough that He is our advocate. There are too many other things to which we should turn our attention. We have no time for concerns of vengeance.

We need to follow the example set forth by our Lord when we feel tempted to foster anger and bitterness toward our adversaries. "When he was reviled, he did not revile in return; when he suffered, he did not threaten, but continued entrusting himself to him who judges justly" (1 Peter 2:23).

Christ entrusted Himself to His Father, who judges justly.

"And he [Eli] said, 'It is the LORD. Let him do what seems good to him'" (1 Sam. 3:18b). Let's do the same.

We've been talking about the way in which God shows His perfect justice to His children, the way He avenges those who afflict us unjustly. What about God's justice to unbelievers—the ungodly, as they're called in the Bible?

Many of us easily understand God's wrath toward "bad people." Just think of all the child abusers, rapists, robbers, murderers, persecutors, wife beaters, pornography producers, and sadistic maniacs out there in the world. Just think of Hitler, Dahmer, Bundy, Manson, Hussein, and bin Laden.

It's no problem to agree with God's wrath toward these types. His wrath can't come too soon for them, can it? We want to say, "Go get 'em, God!"

The Bible gives us examples of the way in which God deals with the Bible's "bad people." In Acts 5, we see His immediate judgment on Ananias and Sapphira. In Numbers 16, we read about His dealing with Korah and his followers. In Acts 12, Herod was the object of God's wrath. In Joshua 7, Achan was found out and utterly destroyed.

Many times we may marvel at the number of "bad people" out there who get away with their crimes—people whom the police or the military might never find. But guess what? God knows where they are. And their punishment is sure. It may not be immediate, but it is inevitable. In this area, we are also to trust His judgment.

The hearts of some are fully given to doing evil. Perhaps that is because they do not see a quickly executed sentence against them. They mistakenly think that they will be able to continue in their vile activities and never get caught. They're utterly wrong about that.

In Ecclesiastes 8:11–13, we read, "Because the sentence against an evil deed is not executed speedily, the heart of the children of man is fully set to do evil. Though a sinner does evil a hundred times and prolongs his life, yet I know that it will be well with those who fear God, because they fear before him. But it will not be well with the wicked, neither will he prolong his days like a shadow, because he does not fear before God."

Yes, we can understand God's wrath to the wicked—that is, those whom *we* view as wicked. It's a little harder for us to wrap our minds around the fact that "the wicked" or "ungodly" are not always "bad" people in the eyes of the world. God also applies these terms to those who do not believe in our Lord Jesus Christ, who do not have—or want—a personal relationship with Him.

For that reason, Christians must have love and compassion for the lost, that we may do everything within our power to bring the message of Christ's salvation to all people. The urgency of this mission becomes clear when we think that our own loved one may be part of this huge group of ungodly ones.

We're told that a vast majority of people will *not* turn to Christ: "Enter by the narrow gate. For the gate is wide and the way is easy that leads to destruction, and those who enter by it are many. For the gate is narrow and the way is hard that leads to life, and those who find it are few" (Matt. 7:13–14).

You see, sinners who refuse to repent and come to Christ are sowing the seeds of their own destruction. Romans 2:5 warns, "But because of your hard and impenitent heart you are storing up wrath for yourself on the day of wrath when God's righteous judgment will be revealed."

We need to understand that if God withholds judgment on sinners until later, He does it for a good purpose. His intention is that His patience, generosity, and long-suffering would serve to entice them to seek salvation. He expresses His goodness to both godly and ungodly for the purpose of leading His enemies to repentance. This principle is taught in Romans 2:4 when Paul asks, "Or do you presume on the riches of his kindness and forbearance and patience, not knowing that God's kindness is meant to lead you to repentance?"

These may be morally good people. They may be zealous and intense followers of other gods. They, too, are considered among the wicked, and their eternal punishment is just as sure. Such a person may be your next-door neighbor, your kindly teacher, your high school classmate—or your son or daughter. We must believe in the righteousness of God's justice toward these people as well. Even when the consequences are hard, we are to trust in Him and know that He exercises His judgment *perfectly*—whether we're in agreement or not!

Ultimately, God's blessing of the righteous is assured. It will be carried out in His own time and in His own way. The Bible never says that evil will not flourish in our world. In fact, it promises that it will! But it also says that God will right all wrongs.

One such passage is found in 2 Peter 2:9: "The Lord knows how to rescue the godly from trials, and to keep the unrighteous under punishment until the day of judgment."

Another is Revelation 20:12–13, 15: "And I saw the dead, great and small, standing before the throne, and books were opened. Then another book was opened, which is the book of life. And the dead were judged by what was written in the books, according to what they had done. . . . And they were judged, each one of them, according to what they had done. . . . And if anyone's name was not found written in the book of life, he was thrown into the lake of fire."

Finally, I cannot leave the subject of God's justice without the example of our Lord Jesus Christ. Those of us who struggle with the "it's not fair" attitude must be reminded of the fact that everything He suffered was indeed unjust. In fact, if there was ever a case of unjust suffering, it was that of Jesus.

Though He had done no wrong, had never committed even one offense against God the Father, He suffered the punishment for the sins of His children. He suffered separation from His Father, ripped willingly from His own glory in heaven, in order to reconcile us to God through His sacrifice.

Now *that* was unfair. And thank God for it! Without it, we could never cross the chasm that sin created between our depravity and the holiness of Almighty God. Jesus was the bridge across that chasm. Praise God.

"Surely he has borne our griefs and carried our sorrows; yet we esteemed him stricken, smitten by God, and afflicted.

But he was wounded for our transgressions; he was crushed for our iniquities; upon him was the chastisement that brought us peace, and with his stripes we are healed" (Isa. 53:4–5).

"For our sake he made him to be sin who knew no sin, so that in him we might become the righteousness of God" (2 Cor. 5:21).

"Have this mind among yourselves, which is yours in Christ Jesus, who, though he was in the form of God, did not count equality with God a thing to be grasped, but made himself nothing, taking the form of a servant, being born in the likeness of men. And being found in human form, he humbled himself by becoming obedient to the point of death, even death on a cross" (Phil. 2:5–8).

"Consequently, he is able to save to the uttermost those who draw near to God through him, since he always lives to make intercession for them. For it was indeed fitting that we should have such a high priest, holy, innocent, unstained, separated from sinners, and exalted above the heavens. He has no need . . . to offer sacrifices daily, first for his own sins and then for those of the people, since he did this once for all when he offered up himself" (Heb. 7:25–27).

No, our sense of justice is not God's. Only He could have come up with a plan by which we could be clothed with righteousness—not our own, but Christ's own righteousness. Was it fair for Christ to do this thing on our behalf? Absolutely not. But He did it because of His great love for us and in obedience to His Father.

We should remember this the next time we are required to do more than the other person, when we get sick right before a long-awaited vacation, when we lose someone we love, or when others seem to get the breaks that we never get. When we're tempted to doubt God, we need to stop feeling sorry for ourselves and instead ask, "How can I glorify God through this?"

Besides, the Bible makes it perfectly clear that suffering is a normal part of the true Christian life. God's justice is higher than our misguided, uninformed, tainted perceptions can comprehend. We should be eternally grateful for that.

"Stricken, Smitten, and Afflicted"

Stricken, smitten, and afflicted, see him dying on the
tree!
'Tis the Christ by man rejected; yes, my soul, 'tis he,
'tis he!
'Tis the long-expected Prophet, David's son, yet
David's Lord;
By his Son God now has spoken: 'tis the true and faith-
ful Word.

Tell me, ye who hear him groaning, was there ever
grief like his?
Friends thro' fear his cause disowning, foes insulting
his distress;
Many hands were raised to wound him, none would
interpose to save;

But the deepest stroke that pierced him was the stroke
that Justice gave.

Ye who think of sin but lightly nor suppose the evil great
Here may view its nature rightly, here its guilt may
estimate.
Mark the sacrifice appointed, see who bears the awful
load;
'Tis the Word, the Lord's Anointed, Son of Man and
Son of God.

Here we have a firm foundation, here the refuge of
the lost;
Christ's the Rock of our salvation, his the name of
which we boast.
Lamb of God, for sinners wounded, sacrifice to can-
cel guilt!
None shall ever be confounded who on him their hope
have built.

—*Thomas Kelly, 1804*

REFLECTION, APPLICATION, AND DISCUSSION QUESTIONS

1. What relevance does the way in which we think about
the justice of God have either negatively or positively to
the "it's not fair" attitude?

2. In what way is Job an illustration of a person having problems with God's justice?

3. What problem was the psalmist wrestling with and almost being destroyed by in Psalm 73?

4. Which biblical statements about the fact of God's justice are most meaningful to you? Review the verses mentioned in this chapter as you make your selections.

5. What is meant by the statement that "righteousness and justice" are part of God's holy nature?

6. Since this is true, what are the implications for our own lives?

7. What are we really doing when we think God is being unjust or unfair? What are we really saying?

8. What standard do we often use for determining what is just or fair?

9. According to Scripture, what is the standard of justice?

10. What are some things that we must keep in mind when evaluating whether an unpleasant circumstance or apparent inequity that God allows to come into our lives is just or not? Review the chapter, noting the various factors that help us understand how the so-called inequities are only *apparent* and not real.

11. What does the example of our Lord Jesus Christ have to do with the justice of God?

12. What does the hymn "Stricken, Smitten, and Afflicted" tell us about the sufferings of Christ?

    a. What words does the hymn use to describe the suffering of Jesus?

b. What does this hymn tell us about who Jesus was and is?

c. What does this hymn suggest we may learn from the sufferings of Christ?

d. What does this hymn suggest are the benefits we receive because of the sufferings of Christ?

13. Have you ever been tempted to question the justice of God in your own life or in the world?

a. When? What were the circumstances?

b. What about these circumstances tempted you to question God's justice?

c. Why do we sometimes question the justice of God? What is happening when we do that?

d. What are the consequences in our lives when we doubt or question the justice of God?

e. What must we do to confront the problem of thinking that God is unjust?

5

THE OMNIPOTENCE AND SOVEREIGNTY OF GOD AND THE "IT'S NOT FAIR" SYNDROME

Sometimes people struggle with the "it's not fair" attitude when they don't truly believe that God is omnipotent or sovereign. They may not believe that He has anything to do with the apparent injustices they face in this world. Instead, they believe that these so-called injustices are caused by men, by Satan, or simply by chance or bad luck. Perhaps they were just in the wrong place at the wrong time.

First, let's define our terms. We've already discussed *omnipresence*, which is God's ability to be everywhere at all times. We've talked about *omniscience*, God's ability to know everything at all times. Now we're discussing *omnipotence*, which is God's ability to be all-powerful, and *sovereignty*, which is His rulership over all things, His absolute authority over everything.

So what is God's role when seemingly unjust events occur? Where is He in all of this? Is He a benevolent Grandfather, who looks on from above, not daring to lift a hand to change things? Is He saddened by our plight, but powerless to do anything about it? Does He throw these things at us just to make us miserable? As in the old-time westerns, is He maliciously shooting at our feet to make us dance?

I have news for you. If God were like that, He would be no God at all and everything in the Bible would be false! If that were true of Him, there would be no need for prayer— what good would it do, after all? There would be no need to study the Bible—how could we trust it, after all? There would be no reason to praise God in song or word—what would there be to praise, after all?

But praise be to God! He is *not* an impotent God, powerless to lift His hand to help us. He does *not* sit on His throne, wringing His hands in sorrow and despair. He does *not* capriciously throw trouble our way just to watch us squirm. No! The God of the Bible is who He says He is!

What God Is *Not*!

Before we delve into the Scriptures to discern the true power and character of Amighty God, let's first look into some false beliefs about Him.

Some people have a *deistic* view of God. That is, they believe He originally created the universe and then created natural laws by which the universe is to be run. According to this view, He then removed Himself from the whole operation and is allowing it to run by itself.

This view of God describes Him as a giant watchmaker, who creates a watch and then merely allows the watch to wind down by itself. He's an interested spectator in the affairs of the world, but not a participant in them.

Another illustration of this errant view of God is that He is like an absentee landowner who made and owns the world, but never visits and doesn't get involved in the nitty-gritty details of what transpires on His property.

One current twist to this deistic view of God is called the *openness of God theory*, which teaches that God has, by His own choice, taken His hands off the affairs of the world. He doesn't know much more about what is going on than you or I. According to this view, God may *guess* about the future, but He really doesn't know and can't actually do anything to control it. God has chosen to limit His knowledge and His control. And since He doesn't know and doesn't control what is happening, He is not responsible for anything! Apparent injustices are certainly not His fault.

Another version of this limited-God concept is that Satan is very powerful and can pretty much do whatever he wants to do. God is powerless, by choice or not, to restrict Satan and his demon cohorts. So whatever injustices there are in the world are ultimately due to the power of Satan and demons over which God has no present control.

Yet another twist to this deistic concept is that God could do something about the apparent injustices in the world if He wanted to. But He doesn't want to interfere with man's freedom. With this view, it just wouldn't be fair to blame God for the unhappy incidents of our lives. No, instead our "it's not fair" syndrome must be directed toward men, or Satan, or mere happenstance.

What about the *atheistic* view? This is the view that says there is no God at all. Therefore, He is in no way responsible for the inequities we see. How can you blame something or Someone who doesn't exist?

At first glance, any of these versions or variations of them might seem to solve the "it's not fair" problem—but they don't! People who hold to any of these views are still beleaguered by the same emotional and relational difficulties as those suffered by believers.

In fact, they struggle with this attitude even more because if they hold to any of these views, they really have no solution to the problem of seeming injustice. There is nothing that they or anyone else, including God, can do about their problems. There is no hope that things will ever be any different. There is no reason to believe that one day there will be a solution to the problem. These people are faced, instead, with utter hopelessness.

WHY WOULD ANYONE WANT TO BELIEVE THESE FALSE VIEWS?

If nothing but hopelessness lurks at the bottom of their thinking, why would anyone hold to these impotent views of God? In the course of counseling, I have uncovered several reasons.

Sometimes they adopt this position by human logic and choice. They reason that if God could prevent these inequities from occurring and doesn't, then He must not be good or loving. So they reason that this must mean that since God *is* good and loving, as we've seen in the previous chapters, then He must not have the power to do anything about it. These people choose a limited-God concept because it seems the only reasonable solution to them.

Others, however, adopt the limited-God concept because of ignorance or misinformation. Perhaps they've been taught erroneous views about God's sovereignty. One thing is for sure—they either have never been taught or have never truly understood the Bible's teaching on the sovereignty of God.

This was certainly true of me in the early stages of my own Christian life. Although I had been a Christian for four years, I can honestly say that I had never heard about the sovereignty of God. I wasn't rebellious; I was just untaught! This has been true as well with many of the people I've counseled.

I remember a woman I counseled several years ago. When she came to me, she was extremely depressed and anxious. She experienced frequent panic attacks, and was increasingly unable to sleep at night. Her heart raced and her mind grabbed hold of repetitive thoughts. She was at the point of leaving her husband when she came to me. Through the assignments I gave her, she was introduced to biblical teaching about God's sovereignty, as well as God's love, wisdom, and justice. Armed with a proper view of God—who He is and how He works in our lives—she was able to be freed of these miserable symp-

~~toms through the work of the Holy Spirit~~. It took some time, but eventually her life smoothed out as she developed more faith and trust in our sovereign Lord.

She became so excited about this great and wonderful truth that she wanted to go back to her church and tell all her Christian friends about God's sovereignty and the impact that knowing this truth had had on her life and could have on theirs. She wanted to buy a whole case of the relevant books I had given to her as homework assignments.

Another case that comes to mind is one involving a man who sought counseling because of severe depression. He lived his life in hopelessness, anger, bitterness, and resentment—especially toward his mother and father because of what they had done to him. Filled with rage, he directed it toward his wife and others. This man believed he had to control others by overpowering them to prove that he was right and they were wrong. Revenge was his ultimate goal. He could see no purpose for what had happened to him. Because of the way he'd been treated by others, he began to think he was ruined for life. He'd even entertained thoughts of suicide.

It was at this time that the Lord saved the man and made him His child. That's what led him to come to me for counseling. The assignments I gave him emphasized God's wisdom, love, justice, and sovereignty, and though he still struggled at first, the man's life was transformed! Almost twenty years later, he is still on track and filled with hope.

Regardless of the reasons you believe what you believe, the solution to these "it's not fair" sorrows is to inundate yourself with solid teaching on these issues and to change your thinking in conformance with God's Word. Through His

Word, He will renew and transform your mind—and with it, your emotions and behavior.

So if you do this, will your world suddenly be a little rosier, will the horrifying events in your life magically disappear, and will the bluebird of happiness perch on your finger when you pull yourself out of bed each morning? No. Sad things are simply that—they're sad. They hurt.

But the way you *think* about these things will change. Looking through this spiritual lens will allow you to drop the burden of confusion and hopelessness. Maybe you'll be able to learn what Paul described when he said, "I know what it is to be in need, and I know what it is to have plenty. I have learned the secret of being content in any and every situation, whether well fed or hungry, whether living in plenty or in want" (Phil. 4:12 NIV). Maybe for the first time in your life, you'll be able to submit to God's authority over your life with joy and praise—and *hope!*

WHAT THE SOVEREIGNTY OF GOD ACTUALLY IS

The sovereignty of God is wise. The sovereignty of God is loving. The sovereignty of God is just. It's a package deal! When we're struggling with "it's not fair," we need to reflect on these important truths about God. They function to reassure us that things are not out of control. Though they may seem chaotic and unmanageable to us, we can rest assured that God holds everything in the palm of His hand and knows what's going on—not only in our lives but in everyone else's. He knows what's happening in every molecule of the universe! So please understand that nothing is out of His control.

This same concept is articulately described in *Trusting God Even When Life Hurts*, by Jerry Bridges:

> All things are indebted for their existence to the continuous sustaining action of God exercised through His Son. Nothing exists of its own inherent power of being. Nothing in all creation stands or acts independently of the Lord's will. The so-called laws of nature are nothing more than the physical expression of the steady will of Christ. The law of gravity operates with unceasing certainty because Christ continuously wills it to operate. The chair I am sitting on while I write these words holds together because the atoms and molecules in the wood are held in place by His active will.
>
> The stars continue in their courses because He keeps them there. Scripture says, "He . . . brings out the starry host one by one, and calls them each by name. Because of his great power and mighty strength, not one of them is missing" (Isaiah 40:25).
>
> God's sustaining action in Christ goes beyond the inanimate creation. The Bible says that He gives life to everything (Nehemiah 9:6). "He supplies the earth with rain and makes grass grow on the hills. He provides food for the cattle and for the young ravens when they call" (Psalm 147:8–9). God did not simply create and then walk away. He constantly sustains that which He created.
>
> Further, the Bible teaches that God sustains you and me. "He himself gives all men life and breath and everything else. . . . 'For in him we live and move and

have our being'" (Acts 17:25–28). He supplies our daily food (2 Corinthians 9:10). Our times are in His hands (Psalm 31:15). Every breath we breathe is a gift from God, every bite of food we eat is given to us from His hand, every day we live is determined by Him. He has not left us to our own devices, or the whims of nature, or the malevolent acts of other people. No! He constantly sustains, provides for and cares for us every moment of every day.[1]

In keeping with what Bridges has written about the meaning and importance of the sovereignty of God in our lives, I want to quote from one section of my book *Down, but Not Out*, which expands on the meaning and implications of knowing and believing in God's absolute sovereignty:

There is a passage in Isaiah 40 that I find especially compelling as a description of the awesome glory of God. Verse 12 asks, "Who has measured the waters in the hollow of His hand, and marked off the heavens by the span, and calculated the dust of the earth by the measure, and weighed the mountains in a balance and the hills in a pair of scales?" These are metaphors, of course, because God is a spirit and does not have a body as we do, but they tell us something of how big God really is. It is awesome to think that all the water of the earth could fit in the hollow of God's hand, and that the universe—which is infinite to us—is shorter than the length of God's hand.

Psalm 33:8 declares, "Let all the earth fear the LORD; let all the inhabitants of the world stand in awe of Him." Most of us do not do enough of that. We are too busy to stand still before our Creator and meditate on His glory and majesty. But in Psalm 46:10 God says, "Be still, and know that I am God; I will be exalted among the nations, I will be exalted in the earth." (NKJV).

Moses needed to be reminded of this when he became greatly discouraged in his role as leader of the Israelites. He had just returned from Mount Sinai after receiving the first tablets of stone. When he came down into the camp of the Israelites, he found them worshipping and sacrificing to a golden calf that Aaron, Moses' assistant, had helped them make. After dealing with the people's sin, praying earnestly for their forgiveness, and pleading with God to not destroy them completely, Moses was understandably discouraged about his role as their leader. He pleaded with God, "Now therefore, I pray You, if I have found favor in Your sight, let me know Your ways that I may know You, so that I may find favor in Your sight. Consider too, that this nation is Your people" (Ex. 33:13). God replied to Moses, "My presence shall go with you, and I will give you rest" (33:14). The Lord reassured Moses that he would never have to do anything by himself or in his own strength.

Moses was not yet satisfied, however, and pressed God for further assurance of His help. He implored God, "I pray You, show me Your glory!" (33:18). God responded by telling Moses that though He could not show Moses His face, "for no man can see Me and live," He would allow Moses to see a small portion of His back (33:19–23). When Moses came down from the mountain after what must have been the most amazing experience of his life, his face shone so brightly that he had to wear a veil in the presence of the Israelites (34:29–30).

God is so glorious that if we in our present bodies were to see His full glory and majesty, we would be disintegrated in His presence. Even the seraphim, who are sinless creatures, always cover their faces and their feet in the presence of God (Isa. 6:2). Our God is *truly awesome*, and in times of discouragement, we need to reflect on His glory and majesty.

We also need to reflect on the fact that He has dominion and authority over everything. Jesus declared, "All authority has been given to Me in heaven and on earth" (Matt. 28:18). Psalm 103:19 says, "The LORD has established His throne in the heavens, and His sovereignty rules over all." Psalm 115:3 teaches, "But our God is in the heavens; He does whatever He pleases."

Our God answers to no one. He is sovereign over the angels, over Satan, and over the demons. Hebrews 1:14 asks, "Are [the angels] not all ministering spirits, sent out to render service for the sake of those who will inherit salvation?" God commands His angels and they obey Him perfectly, absolutely, exclusively, and continuously. Satan is restrained by God as well, and could do no more to Job than God allowed him to do: "Behold, all that he has is in your power, only do not put forth your hand on him" (Job 1:12). We need to remember the extent of God's dominion and authority.

Bunyan illustrated this idea in *The Pilgrim's Progress* when Christian was walking along and encountered two men, Timorous and Mistrust, running in the opposite direction. As these two men passed Christian, they warned him to turn around and go back because there were lions up ahead. Hearing this, Christian was tempted to turn back, but at that point someone else came along. This person said there were lions but added that those lions were securely chained.

The truth here is that God has Satan and his demons on a chain as well. They can do only what God permits them to do and *no more*. We tend to forget that and become frightened by the thought that there are uncontrolled evil beings all around, ready to do us harm. That can be a very discouraging thought! It is not a thought based on truth, however, and if we want to avoid discouragement, we need to focus our minds on truth.

We need to remember again not only that God is in control of all heavenly powers, but that He is our Savior. In other words, He has only good in mind for us. "If God is for us, who is against us?" (Rom. 8:31). In Jeremiah 29:11 God said, "For I know the plans that I have for you, . . . plans for welfare and not for calamity to give you a future and a hope."

This God, our Savior, has all dominion and authority over all powers on earth as well as in heaven. Proverbs 21:1 teaches, "The king's heart is like channels of water in the hand of the LORD; He turns it wherever He wishes." In Daniel 4:35 Nebuchadnezzar declared, "All the inhabitants of the earth are accounted as nothing, but He does according to His will in the host of heaven and among the inhabitants of earth; and no one can ward off His hand or say to Him, 'What have You done?'" There is no one on earth that can call God to account for anything.

We return to Isaiah 40, where verse 15 says, "Behold, the nations are like a drop from a bucket, and are regarded as a speck of dust on the scales." A speck of dust, when we are weighing much more significant items, is not even worth brushing off; that is what God calls all the nations of the earth. All together, they are an insignificant speck in His sight, and He has complete dominion over them.

God is also sovereign over the circumstances of our lives. Joseph told his brothers, who had intended to harm him, "As for you, you meant evil against me, but God meant it for good in order to bring about this present result" (Gen. 50:20). Proverbs 21:30 teaches, "There is no wisdom and no understanding and no counsel against the LORD." And, of course, Romans 8:28 promises, "And we know that God causes all things to work together for good to those who love God."

God has dominion and authority over all His creation as well. He causes the sun to shine (Matt. 5:45) and the rain to fall (Amos 4:7). He controls the lion's mouth (Dan. 6:22). Job acknowledged, "It is God who removes the mountains, they know not how; when He overturns them in His anger; who shakes the earth out of its place, and its pillars tremble; who commands the sun not to shine, and sets a seal upon the stars; who alone stretches out the heavens and tramples down the waves of the sea" (Job 9:5–8).

When we lived in California, we experienced firsthand the Lord shaking the earth out of its place. The earthquake of 1994 was the most frightening thing we have ever experienced in terms of the forces of nature, and it was a great comfort to know that God was in control. My wife was teaching kindergarten at the time, and when the children in her class became frightened by the aftershocks (which continued for days afterward), she calmly explained to them that "God was just settling the earth."

It was not until the principal was in her classroom during a later aftershock that she realized what a comfort this was to her students. As the principal attempted to comfort the students himself, expecting them to be quite frightened by the shaking, several of them reassured him, "Mr. Duncan, don't worry; it's just God settling the earth." Those kids understood that God is in control of the forces of nature, and they were able to minister to their principal at a time when he expected to comfort them.

~~God has all glory, majesty, dominion, and authority; that is a powerfully encouraging truth. Not only that, but Jude said that He has it "before all time and now and forever" (v. 25).~~ Throughout history, there have been rulers with immense power and prestige. When Alexander the Great was twenty-nine years of age, he had conquered all the known world. At that point, it is said that he sat down and wept because there was nothing left to conquer. Alexander the Great might have been great on the earth while he lived, but, as we know, he died and others took his place.

Numerous great kings have reigned on the earth—Nebuchadnezzar, the pharaohs of Egypt, the emperors of Rome—and all of them have died. Nations rise and fall, rulers come and go, but our God reigns! Whatever the military capacity of a nation, even a nation as strong as ours, God's strength is infinitely beyond it. "Some boast in chariots and some in horses, but we will boast in the name of the LORD, our God. They have bowed down and fallen, but we have risen and stood upright" (Ps. 20:7–8).

Previously in this chapter, I intimated that practical implications flow out of knowing and believing in the absolute sovereignty of God, but I haven't yet been as specific as I want to be. So at this point I want to include a list of some of the implications of this proper understanding of God's sovereignty. Think of what impact these great truths should have on your personal life and outlook. Because He is absolutely sovereign:

1. God is accountable to no one!
2. No one has any control over God.
3. He is all-powerful. His power is limitless, infinite.
4. God is able to carry out His holy will in all things.
5. God can do anything that is consistent with His character—holy, wise, loving, and just.
6. God has absolute rule over all His creation for His own glory and the good of His people.
7. God's love always wills what is best for us. His wisdom knows what is best, and He has the power to bring it about. His sovereignty is not exercised capriciously, but in such a way that God in His love deems best for us.
8. God completely upholds and sustains the universe and everyone and everything in it day by day, hour by hour, by the word of His power.
9. No one can thwart His will or act outside the bounds of His will.
10. Nothing is too small or trivial to escape His notice and control. And nothing is so great that it is beyond His power to control it.
11. God works in our hearts and shows us favor when that favor works to accomplish His purposes.
12. God rules over the nations and governments of this world.
13. He determines the person and the times for the rulership of every nation.
14. He rules over the forces of nature.
15. He rules over our physical afflictions and infirmities, our health and fitness.
16. God rules over Satan and his demon cohorts.

The following passages of Scripture illustrate the biblical verification of these sixteen statements I've just made. (Again, as you read the following Bible passages, I encourage you to take the time to meditate on what each of them means and to ask yourself these questions: What impact would such a statement have on me? What would and should be my emotional, behavioral, and attitudinal response to this truth if I really believed it? Don't hurry through them, but do what many scholars think the word *Selah* found in the Psalms is telling us to do—pause and think.)

"Then God said to him in the dream, 'Yes, I know that you have done this in the integrity of your heart, and it was I who kept you from sinning against me'" (Gen. 20:6).

"As for you, you meant evil against me, but God meant it for good, to bring it about that many people should be kept alive, as they are today" (Gen. 50:20).

"But Sihon the king of Heshbon would not let us pass by him, for the LORD your God hardened his spirit and made his heart obstinate, that he might give him into your hand, as he is this day" (Deut. 2:30).

"You are the LORD, you alone. You have made heaven, the heaven of heavens, with all their host, the earth and all that is on it, the seas and all that is in them; and you preserve all of them; and the host of heaven worships you" (Neh. 9:6).

"I know that you can do all things, and that no purpose of yours can be thwarted" (Job 42:2).

"Our God is in the heavens; he does all that he pleases" (Ps. 115:3).

"The heart of man plans his way, but the LORD establishes his steps" (Prov. 16:9).

"The king's heart is a stream of water in the hand of the LORD; he turns it wherever he will" (Prov. 21:1).

"No wisdom, no understanding, no counsel can avail against the LORD" (Prov. 21:30).

"In the day of prosperity be joyful, and in the day of adversity consider: God has made the one as well as the other" (Eccl. 7:14).

"He . . . brings out their host by number, calling them all by name, by the greatness of his might, and because he is strong in power not one is missing" (Isa. 40:26).

"I form light and create darkness, I make well-being and create calamity, I am the LORD, who does all these things" (Isa. 45:7).

"Who has spoken and it came to pass, unless the Lord has commanded it?" (Lam. 3:37).

"The Most High rules the kingdom of men and gives it to whom he will and sets over it the lowliest of men" (Dan. 4:17b).

"He does according to his will among the host of heaven and among the inhabitants of the earth; and none can stay his hand or say to him, 'What have you done?'" (Dan. 4:35b).

"Are not two sparrows sold for a penny? And not one of them will fall to the ground apart from your Father. But even the hairs of your head are all numbered" (Matt. 10:29–30).

"But Jesus looked at them and said, 'With man this is impossible, but with God all things are possible'" (Matt. 19:26).

"And his disciples asked him, 'Rabbi, who sinned, this man or his parents, that he was born blind?' Jesus answered, 'It was not that this man sinned, or his parents, but that the works of God might be displayed in him'" (John 9:2–3).

"For truly in this city there were gathered together against your holy servant Jesus, whom you anointed, both Herod and Pontius Pilate, along with the Gentiles and the peoples of Israel, to do whatever your hand and your plan had predestined to take place" (Acts 4:27–28).

"The God who made the world and everything in it, being Lord of heaven and earth, does not live in temples made by man, nor is he served by human hands, as though he needed anything, since he himself gives to all mankind life and breath and everything. . . . 'In him we live and move and have our being'" (Acts 17:24–25, 28a).

"Oh, the depth of the riches and wisdom and knowledge of God! How unsearchable are his judgments and how inscrutable his ways! 'For who has known the mind of the Lord, or who has been his counselor?' 'Or who has given a gift to him that he might be repaid?' For from him and through him and to him are all things. To him be glory forever. Amen" (Rom. 11:33–36).

"But thanks be to God, who put into the heart of Titus the same earnest care I have for you" (2 Cor. 8:16).

"In him we have obtained an inheritance, having been predestined according to the purpose of him who works all things according to the counsel of his will" (Eph. 1:11).

"For by him [Christ] all things were created, in heaven and on earth, visible and invisible, whether thrones or dominions or rulers or authorities—all things were created through him and for him. And he is before all things, and in him all things hold together" (Col. 1:16–17).

"I charge you in the presence of God, who gives life to all things, and of Christ Jesus . . . to keep the commandment unstained and free from reproach until the appearing of our Lord Jesus Christ, which he will display at the proper time—he who is the blessed and only Sovereign, the King of kings and Lord of lords" (1 Tim. 6:13–15).

"He is the radiance of the glory of God and the exact imprint of his nature, and he upholds the universe by the word of his power" (Heb. 1:3a).

"Now to him who is able to do far more abundantly than all that we ask or think, according to the power at work within us, to him be glory in the church and in Christ Jesus throughout all generations, forever and ever. Amen" (Eph. 3:20–21).

Though you might be tempted to skip over these verses, I urge you to go back and review them one by one. Meditate on what they say. It's true that I want you to think biblically about the character of God; though it is my prayer that He will work in your hearts through the words of this book, I want you to realize that what actually changes hearts is not my words, but God's holy Word. That's why understanding these verses, and the whole text of Scripture, is so vitally important.

When we begin to grasp the intricate way in which the Scriptures all fit together, we finally get a glimmer of understanding about our Lord. Our lives contain things that are certainly unpleasant and difficult. But those things do not make God unfair. They make Him generous and gracious because they happen for our best good and for His ultimate glory.

"Now to him who is able to keep you from stumbling and to present you blameless before the presence of his glory with great joy, to the only God, our Savior, through Jesus Christ our Lord, be glory, majesty, dominion, and authority, before all time and now and forever. Amen" (Jude 24–25).

"Immortal, Invisible, God Only Wise"

Immortal, invisible, God only wise,
In light inaccessible hid from our eyes,
Most blessed, most glorious, the Ancient of Days,
Almighty, victorious, Thy great name we praise.

Unresting, unhasting, and silent as light,
Nor wanting, nor wasting, Thou rulest in might;
Thy justice like mountains high soaring above
Thy clouds which are fountains of goodness and love.

Great Father of glory, pure Father of light,
Thine angels adore thee, all veiling their sight;
All praise we would render; O help us to see
'Tis only the splendor of light hideth thee!

—*Walter Chalmers Smith, 1867*

1. What relevance—positive or negative—does the sovereignty or omnipotence of God have to the "it's not fair" attitude?

2. What does the term *omnipotence* mean?

3. List some unbiblical beliefs that people have about God's sovereignty.

4. Why do people adopt these unbiblical views of God's sovereignty? Describe each reason.

5. What are the consequences of adopting any of these unbiblical views of God's sovereignty?

6. Why is it important to keep in mind the truths about God that we discussed in chapter 4 as we think or talk about the sovereignty of God? What did this chapter mean when it said that we must remember that the sovereignty of God is a package deal?

7. What may happen if we don't keep all of these truths in mind as we think about God?

8. Review the quotation in this chapter from my book *Down, but Not Out* and the quotations from Jerry Bridges' *Trusting God Even When Life Hurts*. What is specifically said about the meaning and importance of the sovereignty of God to the believer?

   a. What do these quotations and the Bible passages on which they are based say about the extent of God's sovereignty?

b. What specific areas are mentioned in connection with God's sovereignty?

9. What specific implications of God's sovereignty are mentioned in this chapter?

10. Can you think of any additional implications not mentioned in this chapter that flow from the truth of God's sovereignty?

11. Review the various passages quoted in this chapter to establish the biblical view of God's sovereignty.

    a. Which of these texts are most meaningful and encouraging to you?

    b. Choose two of these texts, write them out, and work on memorizing them.

    c. When you are tempted to become discouraged or adopt the "it's not fair" attitude toward anything in your life or in the world, choose to fill your mind with the truths from these texts.

12. Review the hymn at the end of the chapter and answer the following questions:

    a. What words does this hymn use to describe who and what God is?

    b. What figures of speech are used to describe who and what God is?

    c. What do each of these words or figures of speech mean? Define each term.

    d. What does this hymn suggest should be our response to the God who is described in the hymn?

13. Have you ever questioned or doubted the loving, wise, and just sovereignty of God?

   a. When? Describe the circumstances.

   b. Why? What was at the root of your questions regarding God's loving, wise, and just sovereignty?

   c. What were the consequences of this questioning?

   d. What should you do from now on when you are tempted to question or forget God's loving, wise, and just sovereignty?

Gal 2:20

6

THE LONG VIEW OF
GOD'S JUSTICE AND
THE "IT'S NOT FAIR"
SYNDROME

What do I mean by the "long view" of God's justice? I mean that:

- We need to commit ourselves to trust God and His Word, believing that His justice will ultimately triumph.
- We must be challenged to remember that God will wreak vengeance on those due to receive it—but in His own time!
- We must be encouraged that because of God's sovereignty, justice is *not* out of control in the here and now.

- Our quiet confidence in God breeds stability and delight throughout the changing scenes of our lives.
- We must reflect on the fact that God knows exactly what is happening—now and in the future—and that He knows what to do to make everything right, not according to our view of "right," but His. He is loving, omniscient, omnipresent, and omnipotent, as well as just.

For over fifty years now, a friend of mine has faced many difficult circumstances. She is still able to rejoice in the Lord. So when she sent me the following poem, I read it with interest. This poem describes why she hasn't developed an "it's not fair" attitude:

> I refuse to be discouraged, to be sad, or to cry;
> I refuse to be downhearted, and here's the reason why.
> I have a God who's mighty, who's sovereign and supreme;
> I have a God who loves me, and I am on His team.
> He is all-wise and powerful; Jesus is His name;
> Though everything is changeable, my God remains
> the same.
> My God knows all that's happening, beginning to the
> end;
> His presence is my comfort. He is my closest friend.
> When sickness comes to weaken me, to bring my head
> down low,
> I call upon my mighty God; into His arms I go.
>
> When circumstances threaten to rob me of my peace,
> He draws me close unto His breast, where all my striv-
> ings cease.

And when my heart melts within me, and weakness
takes control,
He gathers me into His arms and soothes my heart
and soul.
The great "I AM" is with me. My life is in His hand.
The Son of God is my hope; it's in His strength I stand.
I refuse to be defeated; my eyes are on my God;
He's promised to be with me as through this life I trod.
I'm looking past my circumstances to heaven's throne
above;
My prayers have reached the heart of God; I'm rest-
ing on His love.
I give God thanks in everything. My eyes are on His
face;
The battle's His, the victory's mine; He'll help me win
the race.

These are the thoughts of one who has triumphed over
"it's not fair." She has learned to think biblically about the
problems and heartaches of her life. She has learned to apply
the truths with which I began this chapter.

Those truths are the keys God gives us to unlock the cage
in which our self-pity places us. Thinking of those keys now
reminds me of an illustration I used in a previous book.
Though this passage deals with depression, it can easily be
applied to the "it's not fair" syndrome.

John Bunyan described the experience of depression very
accurately and vividly in his well-known allegory, *The Pilgrim's
Progress.* At a certain point in their journey, Christian and his
companion, Hopeful, found themselves on the property of
Giant Despair:

The giant got up early the next morning, and walking up and down his grounds, he spotted Christian and Hopeful sleeping there. Then with a fierce, threatening voice he woke them up and demanded where they had come from and what they were doing on his property. Christian and Hopeful answered shakily that they were pilgrims and that they had lost their way. The giant said, "You have committed an offense against me by trampling in and lying on my property last night. Therefore, you must come with me."

Bunyan shows us here that Christian and Hopeful were captured and controlled by depression. In their minds, they had no choice but to submit because Giant Despair seemed to have them by the throat. Knowing they were guilty of a wrong (trespassing), they were overpowered by their emotions and had little to say in their own defense:

> The giant forced them to walk in front of him until they reached the castle. There he threw them into a very dark dungeon without any light which the two men found disgustingly foul and smelly. They lay there from Wednesday morning until Saturday night without even a crumb of bread. Christian felt doubly sorrowful because it was his ill-advised haste that had brought them into this distress.[1]

Here we see the characteristic lack of appetite and inability to see beyond the moment of people who are experiencing depression. Everything around them seems dark and hopeless.

Bunyan went on to describe how the giant would come down to the dungeon and, without the slightest provocation, beat them unmercifully. Between beatings, the two men would lie helplessly on the floor, unable to move, with barely the strength to grieve their miserable condition. Finally, the giant went down to them with a knife, rope, and poison and advised them to kill themselves by saying, "You choose which means of death you prefer. Why should you choose life, seeing that it involves so much bitterness and pain?" Such is the experience of a person who is severely depressed.

After languishing in the dungeon for some time, Christian reached into his pocket and was surprised to find a key. All the time he and Hopeful had been suffering in the dungeon of Giant Despair, Christian had forgotten about that key. The key, of course, represents the promises of God that Christian knew, but neglected to remember and meditate on. Using the key, Christian was able to open the dungeon door and go through it.

In the same way, we must be prepared to patiently continue to challenge ourselves with the truths of God's Word because our minds tend to forget.

In view of these things, it is plain to see that when we are caught up in the miry pit of "it's not fair," what we need is a *faith lift!* In my own way, that's what I've tried to provide by writing this book—guidance to the lift in faith that God's Word can give to us during our own dark times.

In this book, we've looked into the varied divine attributes of our loving Father. We've reviewed His wisdom, love, power, and justice. The bottom line for us is this: Are we willing to walk by faith? Or do we choose to

~~walk by sight? Trusting our finite sense of reason instead of God's infinite wisdom? Are we willing to believe that God, in His sovereignty, will deal fairly with injustice—now and in the future?~~

~~You see, we *must* trust that God is who He says He is, and can do what the Bible says He can. We need to trust completely in His absolute sovereignty and power.~~

BELIEF IN GOD'S SOVEREIGNTY IS ESSENTIAL

Every biblical truth about God is important for us to know and believe, but none is more important than this truth about God's sovereignty over all things. We can ultimately trust God's justice because He is a sovereign God who can accomplish all His holy will.

We can trust that God will punish the wicked and reward the righteous; that He will deal with all of the inequities that occur in this world not only because He is wise and loving, but because He is sovereign and all-powerful as well.

Jerry Bridges made a shocking statement in *Trusting God* that garnered my attention:

> *If there is a single event in all of the universe that can occur outside of God's sovereign control, then we cannot trust Him.* His love may be infinite, but if His power is limited and His purpose can be thwarted, we cannot trust Him. You may entrust to me your most valuable possessions. I may love you and my aim to honor your trust may be sincere, but if I do not have the

power or ability to guard your valuables, you cannot truly entrust them to me.[2]

Rest assured that God has the wisdom, the desire, and the power to do what Psalm 96:11–13, and a host of other Scriptures, says He will do. Therefore, we can trust His justice because He is sovereign.

"Let the heavens be glad, and let the earth rejoice; let the sea roar, and all that fills it; let the field exult, and everything in it! Then shall all the trees of the forest sing for joy before the LORD, for he comes, for he comes to judge the earth. He will judge the world in righteousness, and the peoples in his faithfulness" (Ps. 96:11–13).

IS "IT'S NOT FAIR" A SIN ISSUE?

When you get right down to it, holding on to "it's not fair" is not only harmful to us. It is downright sinful! Why is it sinful?

1. It challenges the justice of God.
2. It challenges the faithfulness of God's Word.
3. It exhibits a clear lack of faith.
4. It measures circumstances by human standards.
5. It sees only the temporary discomfort.
6. It shifts our focus entirely to ourselves.
7. It is based on a worldly, unbiblical understanding of fairness. We set ourselves up as the judge and jury.
8. It assumes that God is under obligation to perform according to our human standards of fairness.

9. It is based on the idea that we deserve something better than we're getting. It ignores the fact that anything short of hell is more than we deserve.

10. It is based on the assumption that God owes us His blessing, that He is under obligation to treat us the way we want to be treated.

11. It ignores the fact that we are in no position to bargain with God—to use our good deeds to merit blessings as we see fit. We deserve nothing. Therefore, anything that He gives us out of His mercy and love is more than we could hope for. He blesses, or withholds blessings from, whomever He chooses.

THE PARABLE OF THE ELEVENTH-HOUR LABORERS

If there's one parable that strikes a chord of unfairness with the worldly-minded, it's this one. The story is found in Matthew 20:1–15. To summarize, a landowner (who represents God) went out early in the morning (about 6 a.m.) and hired laborers to work in his fields that day. This was a customary practice in biblical times. The laborers agreed to work at the wage he'd offered them. About 9 a.m., he hired some more laborers. Around noon, he hired more. And about 3 p.m., he hired even more. At 5 p.m., he went out and hired still more laborers. Then at 6 p.m., at the end of the day, he called all the laborers to him and paid them all the same amount.

Given these facts, isn't it reasonable, from a human standpoint, that the ones who'd worked all day grumbled over the fact that the others had worked less time—some only an hour—and gotten paid the same amount? That wasn't fair, was it?

This is also one of the points of the parable of the prodigal son in Luke 15. In that parable, the father (again representing God) gave generously to the younger son upon his return, though he had strayed and wallowed in riotous living. The father was so overjoyed at his son's return that he threw an enormous party for him, which angered the older son. Why? Because the older son thought, "That's not fair. He never threw *me* a party, and I've remained loyal all these years and never strayed." That just wasn't fair, was it?

A friend of mine worked as a retail manager in a floor-covering store. Her boss, the owner of the store, hired some men to work in retail. It was my friend's job to teach them product knowledge, and train them to sell, to measure, and to figure jobs. She worked hard to teach them what they'd need to know to do a good job. Then one of them let it slip, while complaining about his salary, that he was making so many dollars a month. My friend, the manager of the department, was making less—and there she was, responsible for training these men. When she confronted her boss about this inequity, he merely explained that they were men who had families to take care of. They *needed* to make more money because of that, he told her. That wasn't fair, was it?

How did the landowner in the first parable deal with this situation? According to Jesus, the landowner responded by saying, "Friend, I am doing you no wrong. Did you not agree with me for a denarius [a unit of money]? Take what belongs to you and go. I choose to give to this last worker as

I give to you. Am I not allowed to do what I choose with what belongs to me? Or do you begrudge my generosity?" (Matt. 20:13–15).

From a worldly standpoint, all these stories—the ancient and the modern-day—demonstrate a situation with an unfair boss. But was he? With spiritual eyes, we're able to see that the boss may have been more generous with some than with others, but that he didn't cheat anyone. It's his property. It's his wealth. It's his store. Doesn't he have a right to be generous with his own money—especially since he didn't slight the one who had worked all day?

The point of the second parable is this: neither of the sons deserved anything from the father. Both were acting as though the father were under obligation to share his wealth with them. He wasn't. He was never obliged to do for the one what he did for the other.

The sons in the story represent us. Our heavenly Father is likewise under no obligation to shower us with any blessings at all! And He is certainly not contractually obligated to do for all His children what He does for one of them!

The older brother is so much like all of us, from time to time. His problem was that he assumed that he deserved to be treated in a particular way. He assumed that the father was under obligation to give him exactly what he had given the younger brother. That relates to us when we think that for God to be just, He must treat us exactly the same way in which He treats everyone else. We fail to recognize that any good thing that any of us receives has not been given to us because we deserve it but because God is gracious and generous to undeserving people.

God isn't being unfair or unjust when He chooses to bestow His undeserved blessings to some people and not bestow certain blessings to others. God is under no obligation to treat all of us exactly alike. If He blesses some people in unusual ways, it is not because they deserve it, but because He has chosen to be generous with what belongs to Him. His generosity serves His purposes—for His glory and for the good of His children.

What about those who have been Christians for fifty or sixty years? Is it fair that they will receive the same salvation as the one just converted? Look at the apostle Paul, who worked tirelessly, selflessly, devotedly, and sacrificially for over thirty years. Then look at the thief on the cross, who never did one thing for Christ's kingdom. He wasn't baptized. He wasn't a member of a church. All he did was believe on Jesus Christ as his Lord and Savior. When he breathed the words, "Jesus, remember me when you come into your kingdom" (Luke 23:42), that's all he needed to ensure a place with Jesus in paradise. Was that fair?

Praise God that His justice is far above our own frail sense of fairness. Because of His great mercy, we who belong to Him are all heirs with Him in the kingdom. There may be degrees of blessing in heaven, but our own presence there is just as surely determined by our loving Father as it is for the greatest Christian who ever lived!

When we hold tight to our "it's not fair" feelings, we need to ask ourselves whether we're looking at our situation through spiritual eyes or worldly ones. God has a right to do with His children as He sees fit.

When we complain against our circumstances and trials, aren't we actually complaining against our Father? Who do we think we are? Sometimes we need to be reminded of just who we are and who God is. We need this reminder when we hold on, like spoiled, petulant children, to "it's not fair."

"It Is Well with My Soul"

When peace, like a river, attendeth my way,
When sorrows like sea billows roll;
Whatever my lot, Thou hast taught me to say,
It is well, it is well with my soul.

Chorus:

It is well with my soul;
It is well, it is well with my soul.

Though Satan should buffet, though trials should come,
Let this blest assurance control,
That Christ has regarded my helpless estate,
And has shed his own blood for my soul.

My sin – O the bliss of this glorious thought! –
My sin, not in part, but the whole,
Is nailed to the cross and I bear it no more;
Praise the Lord, praise the Lord, O my soul!

O Lord, haste the day when the faith shall be sight,
The clouds be rolled back as a scroll,

The trump shall resound and the Lord shall descend;
"Even so" – it is well with my soul.

—*Horatio G. Spafford, 1828–88*

REFLECTION, APPLICATION, AND DISCUSSION QUESTIONS

1. This chapter is entitled "The Long View of God's Justice and the 'It's Not Fair' Syndrome." What is meant by "the long view of God's justice"?

2. Review the poem at the beginning of the chapter and note the reasons given that kept this person from being discouraged.

3. Review the illustration from *The Pilgrim's Progress* and note everything you learn about what happens when a person becomes depressed (which is often a fruit of the "it's not fair" attitude). What was involved in Christian's being released from his depression?

4. What does all of this suggest about how to overcome the "it's not fair" attitude?

5. Review what this chapter says about why the "it's not fair" attitude is a sin.

   a. Do you agree or disagree?

   b. On what basis do you agree or disagree?

   c. Which of the reasons given in the chapter to support the argument that this attitude is a sin are most compelling to you?

d. Which is the weakest argument?

6. Review the parable of the eleventh-hour laborers.

   a. What is the main point of the story?

   b. What other biblical accounts make a similar point?

   c. How is the older brother in the story of the prodigal son like us?

   d. Why is God not being unfair or unjust when He chooses to give something to someone else that He doesn't give to us?

7. According to verse one of the hymn quoted at the end of the chapter, in what circumstances are we to say, "It is well with my soul"?

8. According to verse two of this hymn, what is our "blest assurance" when we're undergoing trials? How does that knowledge buffer us from experiencing the "it's not fair" syndrome?

9. Verse three reminds us of our greatest blessing from our Lord. What is that blessing? Does this blessing evoke praise to the Lord in your heart? How might the remembrance of this sacrificial love support you through your own set of trials?

10. According to verse four, when will our faith become sight? What do you think that phrase means? What effect does this knowledge have on our motivation to exercise faith until that day?

11. What must we do when we are tempted to question God's loving, wise, and just sovereignty?

2 Peter 1:3

7

IMPORTANT REMINDERS FOR OVERCOMING AND PREVENTING THE "IT'S NOT FAIR" SYNDROME

A few things need to be stated at this point. One is that in and of ourselves, we cannot eradicate our tendency toward feeling sorry for ourselves. If we try to do it by our own strength, we will fail repeatedly. We may be able to improve our attitudes a little, but that improvement is often short-lived.

So how can we make *permanent* changes in our thinking? Is this a hopeless pursuit? Not at all. We just need to ask God to change us. We change through His strength, not our own. The Holy Spirit, our great Comforter, equips us with the tools for change. He enables and empowers us to move beyond our human tendencies and stretch our maturity by godly thinking.

In Romans 12:2, Paul instructs: "Do not be conformed to this world, but be transformed by the renewal of your mind, that by testing you may discern what is the will of God, what is good and acceptable and perfect." Therefore, the daily renewing of our minds must be accomplished through the Word of God.

"His divine power has granted to us all things that pertain to life and godliness, through the knowledge of him who called us to his own glory and excellence" (2 Peter 1:3). His Word is the principal tool the Holy Spirit uses to sanctify us. Without it, there is no hope for permanent change or genuine spiritual maturity.

Another tool He uses to mold us into the likeness of our Lord is trial and hardship. Yes, suffering is one of the chief tools in God's tool chest. Through suffering, He shapes us and chisels away all the dross—and through time, we become more like Him.

Todd Murray, the worship pastor at the Bible Church of Little Rock, wrote a song called, "I Am Not Alone." I'd like to quote part of it here because it contains such sound biblical truth:

> I will not resist You when You move Your hand to mold me.
> I will not insist You show me all Your plans today.
> I will not despise the tools You're using now to shape me.
> I will not require understanding to obey.

And I refuse to fear, when the future is unclear,
Knowing You are here close beside me.
When I haven't got a clue what it is that You're up to,
Even then I know that You have not abandoned me.
'Cause faith is believing in things that are yet unseen.
Faith is believing God will intervene.

Pray that God will cause you not to despise the tools He uses to conform you to the likeness of His precious Son. Yes, it may be a painful process—it usually is—but the end result is worth it. Sad to say, most people care more about alleviating the pain of suffering than they do about finding the purpose of God in it.

Another admonition we should remember is this: when we hold on to grudges and seek opportunities to retaliate against those who hurt us, we are victimizing ourselves. We must remember that all vengeance rightly belongs to the Lord. When we forgive others, we give them pardon. Pardon was freely given to us through the sacrifice of Jesus Christ. We are to show others this same grace. If these people do not repent, we must trust that God will take care of the problem. He can bring them to their knees more effectively than we ever could. When we cast our cares on Him, let our grudges against others be one of those cares. We don't need them. God will take care of us.

"And my tongue will talk of your righteous help all the day long, for they have been put to shame and disappointed who sought to do me hurt" (Ps. 71:24). Our battles belong to the Lord. Let's leave them with Him. This attitude of trust demolishes our sinful clinging to "it's not fair."

Many times, people assume that theology is dry and irrelevant. Yet our theology, good or bad, controls our very lives—

our thoughts, attitudes, and behaviors. That's why it's so important to continue to seek the Lord, to strive to gain an understanding of His Word. This book is designed to teach a proper, biblical theology, and I pray that through these efforts, we may be able to throw off the "it's not fair" mentality. Because of His grace, God will remove our envy, bitterness, resentment, revenge, and self-pity.

The mental picture I see is the act of unsaddling a horse. The horse has been burdened by saddle, blanket, and rider for some time. As the rider dismounts, a certain degree of relief is accomplished. But when the weight of that saddle and blanket is also removed, the horse is, at last, free of his burden.

When we hold on to our sinful attitudes, we struggle under our own burdens. No amount of our own bucking against it will dislodge our troublesome load. Instead, it will merely leave us exhausted, frustrated, and beaten down. But if we stand still and know that He is God and trust Him in all things, He graciously removes our burden and takes it away, leaving us free to live unencumbered lives of gratitude and faith.

One attitude of modern thought, though frequently unvoiced, is that God is in charge of the really big stuff, the major things, but it is less clear that He cares about the little things, too. This view, however, is not correct. We can cast *all* our concerns and burdens at His feet. He has commanded us to do so. "Humble yourselves, therefore, under the mighty hand of God so that at the proper time he may exalt you, casting all your anxieties on him, because he cares for you" (1 Peter 5:6–7).

Again, in D. A. Carson's book *How Long, O Lord?* we read:

Yet God is a personal God who responds. . . . The degree of our peace of mind is tied to our prayer life

(Phil. 4:6–7). This is not because prayer is psychologically soothing, but because we address a prayer-answering God, a personal God, a responding God, a sovereign God whom we can trust with the outcomes of life's confusions. And we learn, with time, that if God in this or that instance does not choose to take away the suffering, or utterly remove the evil, *he does send grace and power.* The result is praise; and that, of course, is itself enjoyable, in exactly the same way that lovers enjoy giving each other compliments.[1]

"I Don't Get It!"

We've encountered and examined many truths about God in these pages. But perhaps you still say, "I hear what you're saying, but I just don't get it yet. It makes no sense to me."

Perhaps you should go back to the basics. Deuteronomy 29:29 presents us with the standards for human thinking and curiosity: "The secret things belong to the LORD our God, but the things that are revealed belong to us and to our children forever, that we may do all the words of this law."

So you see, there are some things that we will never be able to understand on this side of heaven. But there are many things that God has revealed to us through His Word. And these are things that belong to us. They *can* be understood. If it were impossible, He wouldn't have bothered to tell us. Again, we're faced with a spiritual tension. We are responsible for learning His Word. But He is responsible to illumine our hearts to understand it.

"So faith comes from hearing, and hearing through the word of Christ" (Rom. 10:17).

Therefore, if you are still slow to understand the truths set forth in the Bible, your recourse is clear. You must throw yourself upon God's mercy and ask Him to open your eyes to His truth. He will not withhold this blessing. It may require little baby steps when you first begin to study His Word. But that tentative beginning will evolve into understanding and confidence in spiritual things.

If you have difficulty understanding these things on your own, seek the wise counsel of others. I can't begin to count the ones who have come to me for this very reason, and time and again, the Lord has been faithful to grant understanding, and with it a kind of joy that these people have never experienced—the joy of the Lord!

The Word was not given merely for academic or speculative purposes. It is alive and nurturing. It illumines and transforms. Our understanding of it is vital to the quality of our lives and of our worship.

WHOSE STANDARD ARE WE TO USE?

Sometimes we're tempted to think of God and to judge Him by our standards. The reason behind this is the sin from which all other sins flow—*pride*. When we use our own thoughts as the perfect standard, we're engaged in sinful, prideful thinking.

And the Bible is not served to us cafeteria-style. We don't get to pick and choose what we want. If we adopt only those parts of the Bible that we feel comfortable with, we are in desperate danger of creating a god in our own image. It's wrong, but we still do it. Yet God repeatedly reminds us throughout the Bible that we were created in *His* image and not the other way around.

"You thought that I was one like yourself" (Ps. 50:21). The implication is, "Well, I'm not!"

A beautiful example of this truth appears in Hosea 11. For ten chapters, we're told about the unfaithfulness of Israel to God. Time and time again, the people turned from Him. Time and time again, they dishonored Him. Finally, in chapter 11, we see a different side of God.

"When Israel was a child, I loved him, and out of Egypt I called my son" (11:1). Here Israel is characterized as God's little child and God as the loving Father. "The more they were called, the more they went away; they kept sacrificing to the Baals and burning offerings to idols. Yet it was I who taught Ephraim [Israel] to walk; I took them up by their arms, but they did not know that I healed them. I led them with cords of kindness, with the bands of love, and I became to them as one who eases the yoke on their jaws, and I bent down to them and fed them" (11:2–4).

What a sweet image we see of Almighty God. I can't help remembering when my own children were small. Perhaps you had this experience as well. Remember when they held tightly to your fingers as you taught them to walk? That's the picture that God paints here for us. He has tenderly taught His nation to walk. He has bent down to remove the people's yoke of bondage and to give them food, nurturing them. In His righteous anger, He warns them, "They shall not return to the land of Egypt, but Assyria shall be their king, because they have refused to return to me. The sword shall rage against their cities, consume the bars of their gates, and devour them because of their own counsels. My people are bent on turning away from me, and though they call out to the Most High, he shall not raise them up at all" (11:5–7).

He would have been perfectly within His rights to carry out this ruling, too! Who could blame Him for raining judgment on His unfaithful children? They have obviously grieved Him without repentance! We've seen specific examples of it for ten chapters in Hosea. As we read about their unfaithfulness to their loving Father, we're tempted to say, "Go get 'em, God! They deserve everything You do to them! How dare they disrespect You like this?"

And just as we prepare to read about His wrath destroying them, instead He says, "How can I give you up, O Ephraim? How can I hand you over, O Israel? . . . My heart recoils within me; my compassion grows warm and tender. I will not execute my burning anger; I will not again destroy Ephraim; for I am God and not a man, the Holy One in your midst, and I will not come in wrath" (11:8–9).

Did you catch that line? "I am God and not a man." If it were up to us, we'd squash them underfoot. We'd punish them for turning against us. But wait . . . aren't we just like them? Don't we turn from our God over and over again? Aren't we faithless while He continues to be faithful?

Oh, thank You, God, for not being like us. Thank You, God, that You are God and not a man. Because of Your mercy and continuing love for us, You refuse to drive us away in Your righteous anger!

Instead, for those of us who are indeed His children, He gives us grace. He shows us undeserved kindness and protection. His love, His thoughts, His justice, and His mercy are above all we can fathom.

And yet this is the God we blame for being unfair?

In *Sunsets: Reflections for Life's Final Journey*, the author describes a scene between the teenage daughter of a man dying of cancer and her worship pastor:

"Why, Alex? Why is He letting this happen to Daddy? Can you answer that? I'm praying and praying, and nothing is happening. He's not getting any better! . . ."

"Who says He isn't answering your prayers?"

"Well, Daddy's still sick, isn't he?"

"Then there's your answer. The answer is not always yes, Laura. Sometimes the answer is no. You seem to be losing sight of some things that I think you know. The first is that God is not absent here. He is present. He is in control of everything that happens."

"Humph," she snorted as she rolled her eyes at Alex. . . .

Alex continued, "Do you want a God who's like some kind of genie in a bottle? You rub your hands together three times, and He grants all your wishes. He's all-powerful but subject to your whims and desires. A God who's under your control. Do you want a God who only does what you tell Him to do? In that case, who's God?"

Laura said nothing. She just looked at him through eyes brimming again with tears. Her lower lip trembled. She started to say something, then thought the better of it, and finally looked down at her hands.

"Laura, is that the kind of God you want? I don't. I'm glad I have a God who is SO BIG that sometimes He does stuff that I might not even understand. We have faith that what He does, He does because He loves us. We are told that whatever He brings into our lives will ultimately be for our good. Even when we don't understand. Even when we don't like it. That's what trust is all about!"[2]

Like impetuous children, don't we bombard God with doubts and obstinate suspicions, as Laura did? Don't we sometimes want a God who will do what we say? And when we don't get our way, what is our response—a mature trusting in Him, or pouting and blaming Him for being unfair? We need to ask ourselves these questions when we respond to Him with our childish attitudes and behaviors.

Romans 13:14 teaches us, "But put on the Lord Jesus Christ, and make no provision for the flesh, to gratify its desires." Our concerns should be the fulfillment of *God's* will, not our own. A sweet truth is that when we do this, we increasingly realize that His will *has become* our will!

Suffice it to say that we can never fully understand the mind of God. If God were fully understood, He would be . . . well, finite—like us! He would not be worthy of our trust, our praise, or our worship. We can worship only a God who transcends mere human understanding.

When we refuse to believe in God until we are satisfied, *our* mind becomes the standard. That is sinful thinking. When we attempt an understanding that is beyond finite ability, we are foolish. That is futile thinking. Let us instead discover the richness and wisdom of godly thinking.

CONCLUSION

Sometimes it's tempting for us to blame God as we hold fast to our "it's not fair" thinking. But God tells us in His Word that temptations can be overcome. He's provided a way through them.

"No temptation has overtaken you that is not common to man. God is faithful, and he will not let you be tempted beyond your ability, but with the temptation he will also provide the way of escape, that you may be able to endure it" (1 Cor. 10:13).

"For we do not have a high priest who is unable to sympathize with our weaknesses, but one who in every respect has been tempted as we are, yet without sin. Let us then with confidence draw near to the throne of grace, that we may receive mercy and find grace to help in time of need" (Heb. 4:15–16).

What lessons can we learn from these passages?

- In Jesus Christ is One who has experienced every temptation you have.
- He is your Great High Priest, interceding for you with God.
- He understands your difficulties because He Himself faced the most severe difficulties—all undeserved!
- And yet He did not sin!
- You are encouraged to go boldly to Him, seeking His mercy and help.

- He will give you all you need.
- He knows all you are going through in this world.
- As a result, He can sympathize with you.
- Though the temptation seems strong, God will always provide a way of escape. Many times we don't find that escape because we don't look for one.
- Take your problems to Him:
  - In the proper spirit (boldly).
  - With large expectations of mercy and help.
  - Knowing that these will be given precisely when needed, not before or after.

Previously I said that our *working* (not abstract) theology determines the way in which we think, feel, and behave. The reverse is also true: the way in which we think, feel, and behave reveals our real theology (i.e., our belief system).

One last question I wish to ask is this: what is your chief goal in life? If your chief goal is the pursuit of personal happiness and enjoyment, I can guarantee that you *will* be disappointed, frustrated, and bewildered. No, it's not because I'm some kind of prophet who sees into the future. Instead, I can make this prediction because I've spent my life talking to people about their most intimate thoughts. Empirically, I have repeatedly seen this happen. I know what I'm talking about! But more than that, I know the Bible. It tells me what our chief aim should be.

"You shall love the LORD your God with all your heart and with all your soul and with all your might" (Deut. 6:5).

". . . my chosen people, the people whom I formed for myself that they might declare my praise" (Isa. 43:20–21).

"But seek first the kingdom of God and his righteousness" (Matt. 6:33).

"A new commandment I give to you, that you love one another: just as I have loved you, you also are to love one another. By this all people will know that you are my disciples, if you have love for one another" (John 13:34–35).

"Whoever says he abides in him ought to walk in the same way in which he walked" (1 John 2:6).

These verses direct our focus not on ourselves, but on God. Our life is to be lived for *Him*.

"Sadly such teaching seems far removed from the outlook that prevails in large parts of the Church today. The impression is given that the purpose of the Christian life is enjoyment. Everything that stands in the way of that is to be eliminated. People are looking for a problem-free Christianity."[3]

No, our chief aim is not to please ourselves. Our aim is to live a life pleasing to the God who rescued us from destruction and brought us into His marvelous light. If our aim is to please and glorify Him, it changes the way we view the circumstances in our lives. It cures us of wanting to cry "foul" because of what God is bringing us through. We begin to recognize that though we cannot see the future, we know the God who *controls* the future, and it is on Him we can rely.

A train enjoys maximum freedom as long as its wheels remain on the tracks. The same is true of every child of God. God's will can be compared to those train tracks. We enjoy our maximum freedom when we follow the tracks that God sets out for us. When we balk at the degree of incline or the darkness around us, we may get off the tracks of God's will for us. When that happens, we can go nowhere. That is, until we get our footing solidly placed on our tracks again. That's when we know that we can trust Him—wherever His sovereign will takes us.

Through the grace and strength of God, may we keep our wheels on track and our eyes firmly fixed on His face.

Recently, I received a letter from a former student of mine. I include it here because it beautifully illustrates the practical value of knowing and believing the truths about the wisdom, love, justice, and sovereignty of God presented in this book. In the letter this woman mentions some of the very difficult recent experiences in her life, but she also demonstrates how her view of God has preserved her from an "it's not fair" attitude and enabled her to respond positively and productively to the apparent inequities in her life. She writes:

> My family still resists God's pull, but the Lord has increased His pressure on them recently. I was diagnosed with acute myelogenous leukemia. That was at the end of June, and then I was hospitalized for about a month while they administered chemotherapy. They continue to try to kill the cancer in my bone marrow without killing me. God has blessed me exceedingly, abundantly through this whole experience. My church has been such a blessing, and I saw God work in so many ways. Everyone who came in my hospital room was startled by the number of cards I received. I had taped the over two hundred cards up on the walls. So many Christians prayed for me that the time in the hospital was the worst of times and the best of times. That may sound weird, but even when I thought I might be passing with 104.5 fever one evening and I

couldn't breathe, I knew He was right there. It was so sweet to be so conscious of being in His presence. I got to minister to doctors and nurses as well as seeing a neighboring patient come to the Lord through the ministrations of the people in the church. God is so awesome, especially when we rely on Him rather than ourselves. I love being the audience to His mighty work. Ah, but I did have to come home and accept limitations. The doctor forbade me [from] going kayaking when I got bitten by a spider while paddling. My oncologist's favorite phrase when in my presence is, "Karen, Karen, Karen." In all this I have not had any but very minor pain, and I am so grateful for that. I continue to counsel at my church, although on a very limited basis.

Does what we know and believe about God make a difference in the way we live life? In the way we respond to trials? The Bible clearly says it does, and this woman's testimony, along with the testimonies of thousands of others from the past and present, is living proof of that difference.

Knowing and believing these things about God will not preserve you from the difficulties and apparent inequities of life. God never promised they would, but I can guarantee you that they will help you handle what comes into your life, whether pleasant or painful, in such a way that He will be glorified and you will be kept from the "it's not fair" attitude and all the resulting unpleasant and destructive emotions and behaviors that follow as surely as night follows day.

As I write this book, I pray that God would use its contents to cause your love to "abound more and more, with knowledge and all discernment, so that you may approve what is excellent, and so be pure and blameless for the day of Christ, filled with the fruit of righteousness that comes through Jesus Christ, to the glory and praise of God" (Phil. 1:9–11).

"Sovereign Ruler"

His decree who formed the earth
Fixed my first and second birth;
Parents, native place, and time,
Planned within God's loving mind.
He that formed me in the womb,
He shall guide me to the tomb;
All my times shall ever be
Ordered by His wise decree.

Times of sickness, times of health;
Times of poverty and wealth;
Times of trial and times of grief;
Times of triumph and relief.
Times the tempter's power to prove,
Times to taste the Savior's love;
All must come, and last, and end,
As shall please my heavenly Friend.

Chorus:
Sovereign Ruler of the skies,

Ever gracious, ever wise,
All my times are in your hand,
All events at your command.
Sovereign Ruler of the skies,
You are gracious, You are wise,
All my times are in your hands,
All events at your command.

—*John Ryland, 1777*

REFLECTION, APPLICATION, AND DISCUSSION QUESTIONS

1. This chapter asserts that overcoming and preventing the "it's not fair" attitude will require making some changes.

    a. As we think about making changes, what danger must we avoid?

    b. What must we keep in mind as we seek to make the necessary changes?

2. What tools does the Holy Spirit use to make changes in our lives? Gods Word & Trials

3. How is blaming others and even retaliating verbally or passively (or any other way) a way of victimizing ourselves?

4. What are the essential truths taught by Deuteronomy 29:29?

5. What application or relevance does the teaching of this verse have to the "it's not fair" attitude?

6. According to this chapter, how are we often tempted to think of and judge God?

7. What is the basic reason that we do this?

8. According to this chapter, one of the fundamental things we need to learn about God and ourselves is that He is God and we are not. Reflect on this statement based on Psalm 50:21 and Hosea 11:8–9 and think through the impact that this truth should have on us when we think about God and His ways.

   a. How should this truth be an encouragement to us?

   b. How should this truth be a warning to us?

9. When we refuse to believe in God until we are satisfied and fully understand everything perfectly, what are we really doing?

10. Review 1 Corinthians 10:13 and Hebrews 4:15–16 and delineate their important lessons about handling the apparent inequities of life.

11. What is meant by the statement that "the way in which we think, feel, and behave reveals our real theology"?

12. What do you think I meant when I spoke of our "working theology"? What is the difference between an abstract and a working theology?

13. How does the way in which we respond to the apparent inequities of life reveal what we really believe at the point when we respond? How does the way we respond reveal what our real goal in life is?

14. What should be our real goal in life?

15. Review the hymn quoted at the end of the chapter and answer the following questions:

    a. What truths about God are presented in this hymn? List them.

    b. What effect should these truths have on our lives if we really know them and believe them?

    c. What effect have these truths had on your life?

16. Reflect back on everything that you have learned from reading and studying this book and record:

    a. The most important lessons you have learned.

    b. The ways in which you have been convicted.

    c. The ways in which you have been encouraged.

    d. How you will use these truths in your ministry to others.

    e. What you plan to do in response to the lessons you learned, conviction you felt, and encouragements you received and when and how you will communicate these truths in your ministry to others.

Psalm 23

8
_____

THE PRACTICAL VALUE
OF A RIGHT VIEW OF
GOD VERSUS THE "IT'S
NOT FAIR" SYNDROME

This book has asserted that knowing and believing the
truths about God can have a practical impact on our lives.
The following fictional scenarios have been included in this
book to illustrate the responses of a person undergirded with
these truths in contrast with the responses of a person who,
though she says she believes in Christ, either does not know
or does not believe all the truths presented in this book.

The individuals described and their reactions are com-
posites of people I've encountered in ministry. I've known people who responded to difficult situations in exactly the same

way in which these characters do. So in that sense they are real, but not actually representing specific individuals. One is a woman I'm calling Camilla with a husband I've named Freddie; the other is a woman I'm calling Laura with a husband I've named Josh. I want to show you two separate responses to the same set of circumstances.

CAMILLA'S STORY

I'll begin with a paraphrase of the way in which Camilla and many others would rewrite Psalm 23 to reflect the way they think about and live life:

> The LORD is my shepherd; but I want so much more.
>> He makes me lie down in green pastures, but I'm not fond of grass.
> He leads me in paths of righteousness for his name's sake, yet righteousness is really not much fun, you know.
>
> When I walk through the valley of the shadow of death,
>> I will be very afraid,
> though I'm told you're always there with me;
>> your rod and staff,
>>> they don't really comfort me in a time like this.
> What I really need is for you to get me out of here!
>
> You prepare a table before me
>> in the presence of my enemies,
>>> but I'm too intimidated by them to eat;

you anoint my head with oil, though I just washed
   my hair;
   my cup is half empty.
You promised me goodness and mercy
   all the days of my life, but I don't see it.
Yet in spite of my lack of faithfulness,
   I shall dwell in the house of the LORD forever.

A Brief Description of Camilla's Background

Camilla went to church as a child and young adult. At
a young age, she made a profession of faith in Christ. Eventually, she chose to marry a boy named Freddie from her college. He was an unbeliever, but she didn't think that would
make much difference. They loved each other, after all. After
they'd been married a couple of years, they started trying to
have a baby. In the course of three years, she miscarried four
times. Freddie began spending more and more time away from
home. Camilla heard a rumor that he was having an affair
with a girl he worked with. Camilla prayed that God would
give her a child. She was sure the child would bring her and
Freddie closer together again. Now she's almost five months
pregnant, but they've found out that the child has serious birth
defects.

A Brief Description of Camilla's Response to the Difficul-
ties in Her Life

When Freddie, Camilla's husband, discovered that the
child in her womb had serious birth defects, he became furi-
ous with Camilla, though he could not explain why. It was as
though it were her fault that the baby was not right. They'd
waited all this time, and now they were going to have some

kind of little monster. He's angry and Camilla is devastated. She can't believe God is doing this to them. Instead of bringing them together as she had hoped, this baby seems to be tearing them apart. Freddie wants her to have an abortion immediately, but the doctors say that the baby is too far along for that. Freddie has started staying out all night and doesn't answer his cell phone when Camilla tries to call him. She's scared and alone.

Hour after hour she sits around, thinking about how bad she has it. She feels hopeless and has no idea how she will ever be able to cope with what the future holds. She can't imagine what she's done to deserve this. In the past, she seldom read her Bible, and now she reads it even less. She doesn't feel like doing it; besides that, what good has it ever done, and what good would it do now? She thinks that the Bible has never really helped her before and that it's not going to help her now. Since Camilla married Freddie, her church attendance has been very sporadic. Freddie has refused to go with her except on special occasions, and even then, Camilla has felt she was dragging him along. It's easier just to stay in bed on Sunday morning with the newspaper, the TV turned to the news channel, and fresh hot coffee beside them on the table. Besides, with all this going on, the last place she feels like going is to church. Those people don't have problems like these. They wouldn't understand what she's going through.

Before she found out about the baby, she used to pray from time to time—especially when she found herself in some kind of trouble. Now she doesn't even want to pray because she's so angry with God. She tried a couple of times, but all she did was complain to Him and then ask Him to miraculously change her situation to the way she wants it to be.

She simply can't understand why God would allow this to happen to her. She asks over and over: *What did I do to deserve this? Others have good marriages and loving husbands and healthy children. Why not me?*

Sometimes she looks to the heavens and tears just begin to stream down her face. Her only relief comes from watching television for long periods, distracting her mind from her problems—but even that doesn't really help because her protruding stomach is a constant reminder of how awful her life is. She spends time with certain friends, and when she doesn't feel like going to their houses, she spends hours on the phone with them. But she seeks out the ones who will give her the most sympathy and comfort and agree that what's happening to her is not fair. In fact, none of them can figure out or give her any suggestions about why God may be allowing this to happen to her. These friends just commiserate with her and basically tell her that what is happening to her "stinks." She comes away from conversations feeling temporarily better because others agree with her about how horrible the situation is, but in the long run she soon feels even worse because they give her no hope or positive suggestions.

At times, Camilla has even wondered whether she could do something to make the baby die without hurting herself in the process. Perhaps she could fall down the stairs or take some kind of pills that would cause the baby to abort. Her reasoning is that if the baby died, perhaps Freddie might feel sorry for the way he's acted and start loving her again.

As the pregnancy progresses, Freddie tells her that as soon as the baby is born, he's leaving. He has asked Camilla for a divorce and told her he just can't handle it anymore. He thinks it best for them to just move on with their separate lives. Camilla is devastated emotionally and bitter against God. She is angry, fearful, depressed, and ready to give up on God and church. She looks into the future and sees nothing but gloom and doom. And in reference to spiritual things, her thoughts are: *What good does believing in God and going to church do? All I hear is Romans 8:28. Well, how can this possibly work out to my good? Maybe God doesn't love me. Maybe He's punishing me for something. But what? Nothing I've done justifies putting me through this.*

LAURA'S STORY

We begin the Laura story by quoting the real Psalm 23 the way God wrote it through David and the way Laura and others believe it and live it as they face the unpleasant and painful experiences of life:

> The LORD is my shepherd; I shall not want.
> He makes me lie down in green pastures.
> He leads me beside still waters.
> He restores my soul.
> He leads me in paths of righteousness for his name's sake.
>
> Even though I walk through the valley of the shadow of death,
> I will fear no evil,

for you are with me;
>your rod and your staff,
>they comfort me.

You prepare a table before me
>in the presence of my enemies;
you anoint my head with oil;
>my cup overflows.
Surely goodness and mercy shall follow me
>all the days of my life,
and I shall dwell in the house of the LORD forever.

The scenario for Laura represents the way in which a person who really knows and believes in the true and living God handles and responds to the unpleasant and painful circumstances of life.

A Brief Description of Laura's Background

Laura grew up in a Bible-believing church. In her teenage years she came to know Christ as her Lord and Savior. She married a young man from her youth group named Josh who had been her friend for many years. Josh had also been drawn to Christ as a teenager. Both of them are part of a church where God's Word is faithfully preached. After they'd been married a couple of years, they started trying to have a baby. In the course of three years, Laura miscarried four times. During their married life, Josh never wavered in his affection for Laura and showed love and consideration to her as she went through the hardships and disappointments of the miscarriages. Rather than have Laura suffer the disappointment of another miscarriage, Josh even suggested that they adopt instead of continuing with these painful attempts to have a baby. Both of them made this an object of prayer and asked for God's leading. Soon, to their surprise and a little concern, Laura became pregnant. But this time, it appeared that she was going to carry the child and not miscarry. In fact, the child in her womb is now almost five months along. But through the sonograms they discover that this child has serious birth defects.

Laura and Josh's Response to Their Difficulties

When Josh heard the news about the baby's condition, he was disappointed, for sure. They'd waited so long and prayed so fervently for a child, and now that it seemed it was going to happen, he had just assumed the baby would be healthy. Laura cried when she heard the news. Josh squeezed her hand, though, and later told her that whatever happened, with God's help, they would go through this together.

Together they turned to the Bible for strength and comfort. Together they read and discussed passages such as Psalm 23, Psalm 34, Psalm 46, Psalm 103, Psalm 139, Isaiah 40:12–31, and Romans 8:28–39, which speak of God's wisdom, compassion, loving-kindness, omnipresence, and power. They drew instruction about difficult situations from Philippians 1:12–26, Philippians 4:6–9, and the examples of others in Scripture, such as Joseph, Lot, Jeremiah, Daniel, and Paul, who had gone through extremely unpleasant and painful circumstances.

Together Josh and Laura recalled evidences of God's goodness to them throughout their lives. They looked back and received encouragement from the many examples of God's deliverance in their own lives when they were going through other times of great turmoil.

Together they reflected and meditated on the great scriptural truths about God's being so wise that He could never make a mistake. They reminded themselves from Scripture that God is so loving that He would never do anything that was ultimately unkind to His children. They reflected on the fact that because God is holy and righteous, He could and would never do anything that was unjust or not right. They filled their minds with biblical truths about God's power and sovereignty and reminded each other that because God was sovereign, nothing could ever happen that He could not prevent or that was beyond His control. They were encouraged by the remembrance that God's sovereignty was not capricious or arbitrary but rather a loving, wise, and just sovereignty.

They claimed the promises of verses such as Isaiah 41:10, Romans 8:28, and 1 Corinthians 10:13, often repeating them to themselves and each other. They poured out their hearts to God and asked Him for wisdom, strength, and courage. They often followed the counsel of Psalm 46:10 and paused to remember that He is God and also to think about the kind of God that Jesus Christ and the biblical writers say He is.

When one of them was down, the other would seek to encourage and build up that person with love and compassion and review the truths and promises of God's Word. In this situation they didn't simply react. Basically, they became proactive in choosing to think and do the constructive and godly thing even though at times they didn't feel like doing it. They reasoned that since this trial was not a mistake, it was designed for their lives. And though they couldn't see it as a real blessing, they trusted that this was happening for a specific reason that God was bringing into their lives. They knew that He had chosen them to be the parents of this little one and vowed that they would be the best parents possible—even when it was hard.

Yes, Josh and Laura were tempted to be fearful about what the future might hold. Indeed, they were disappointed and frightened at the prospect of having a child with serious disabilities. They definitely had their down times. Yes, they were realistic about the challenges that were before them, and were concerned about what all of this would mean for them and for the child. They didn't try to convince themselves that everything was "peachy keen" and that this was exactly the way they would have wanted it to be. There were times when they wept, but at the same time they found God to be their refuge and strength, their very present help in the time of trouble.

They waited on the Lord again and again—and just as He promised in Isaiah 40:31, their strength was renewed. They were able to mount up with wings as eagles, to run and not be utterly weary. They found comfort in knowing that they had a High Priest in Jesus, who was at the right hand of God interceding for them, and that their Savior had been tempted in all points as they were (Heb. 4:14–15). They rejoiced that He'd invited them to come boldly to His throne of grace to receive mercy and grace in their time of need (Heb. 4:16; 7:25).

They chose to believe that their wise, loving, just, and sovereign God had a purpose and that He would never give them more than they could bear (1 Cor. 10:13). They knew that He would never abandon them (Matt. 28:20b; Heb. 13:5–6). And so through their tears and sorrow, they learned to hope and even rejoice in their God (Phil. 4:4). Day by day, though the circumstances didn't change and though at times they struggled and even failed, in the overall picture they found strength and comfort and hope in knowing and believing in the true and living God who is revealed in the living Word (Jesus Christ) and the written Word (the Bible) (2 Cor. 4:16–18).

Josh and Laura didn't understand exactly why God was bringing them through this trial, yet they were confident that He would bring them through. They learned, by faith, to give thanks for this baby He'd given them—their special gift (Eph. 5:20; Phil. 4:6; 1 Thess. 5:18). They knew that hard times were ahead for all three of them, but they trusted that God had orchestrated all this for their good and for His glory.

When Laura felt the baby move for the first time, she cried tears of joy and called Josh immediately to tell him the news. And together that night, they thanked God again for this baby. With Josh's hand on her belly, Laura had to laugh at the silly, joyful expression on his face when he felt the tiniest little motion.

When Josh and Laura shared the details of the situation with their Christian friends at church, their friends responded with compassion, concern, and encouragement, and when it was appropriate, they reinforced and expanded what Josh and Laura already knew about God and His plans and provisions. Some even volunteered to help out when the new parents needed a little relief from the intense care that the baby would require. Instead of blaming God or yielding to the temptation to think and even say, "It's not fair," Laura and Josh honestly poured out their fears, concerns, and struggles to God and followed the commands of Scripture to bless the Lord at all times (Ps. 62:8; Isa. 50:10; Phil. 4:6).

Together they counseled with one of the pastors of their church and asked him for biblical help about how they should think about the situation and what they should do. Together they continued to be involved in various church activities and to serve in the ways that they had previously served.

Regardless of their circumstances, they knew that God would be faithful to His promises to them as His children. And they knew that this baby would still be the fruit of their union together and therefore precious. They understood that their loving, wise, just, and sovereign heavenly Father intended this child, as well as all other children, as a reward—a blessing—to them and other people (Ps. 127:4–5). So they committed themselves to do their best, with God's promised help, to bring the child up in the discipline and instruction of the Lord and to live their lives to the glory of God. They chose to believe, as Jesus said of the person born blind (born with a handicap) in John 9:3, that God had planned what was happening to them and their child, that the works of God might be displayed in them. This little baby was formed by God exactly the way He designed it to be. They comforted themselves in the remembrance of Psalm 139:13, "For you formed my inward parts; you knitted me together in my mother's womb." No, God doesn't make mistakes.

THE REST OF THE STORY

Laura couldn't seem to concentrate on the words before her. She was distracted by the baby's wriggling within her. As she loved to do, she placed her hand over her belly so that she could feel each little kick and smiled quietly to herself.

The woman next to her eyed her resentfully. Laura didn't know why. She thought to herself that she was probably misinterpreting the woman's expression.

Camilla, the woman next to Laura, thought to herself, "Humph! This woman has a perfect little baby. She has reasons to smile. Not me."

Just then, Tonya, their obstetrician's nurse, walked out to speak softly to another woman in the waiting room. Turning to go back into the office, she noticed Laura and Camilla sitting next to each other in the crowded waiting room.

Tonya blurted, "How odd that you two would be sitting together! Do you know each other?"

Laura and Camilla looked at each other and then at Tonya. Both shook their heads.

"Oh, well. That's weird," Tonya said as she disappeared behind the closing door.

Once more looking at each other, Laura quietly said, "I wonder what she meant by that. Do you have a clue?"

"Nope. Not a clue," Camilla replied.

"Is this your first baby?" Laura asked, trying to be friendly.

Camilla nodded, rolling her eyes.

"And maybe my last," she said jokingly.

But Laura didn't think of it as a joke. Laura wondered why the woman didn't seem to be very happy about this baby. None of her business, she supposed, and turned her eyes back to her book.

Camilla, feeling a little bad about her response, asked, "How far along are you?"

"A little over five months."

"Really? Me, too," Camilla offered. "Is this your first one, too?"

"Yes," Laura said with a smile.

"Yeah, we waited a long time to get pregnant, and now we are! But my baby has a bunch of birth defects and stuff," Camilla shared, her voice hushed and sorrowful.

"Well, I think maybe I know why Tonya said what she said. We're in the same boat, it seems. Our baby has defects, too."

"But you seem so happy!" Camilla exclaimed.

"Well, I am! Aren't you? Why shouldn't I be joyful? This baby is the answer to our prayers, and the way I see it, God chose us out of all the other parents in the world to take care of this little one. I wouldn't have planned it this way, mind you, but then I'm not God, am I?" Laura smiled.

Camilla couldn't believe what she was hearing and seeing.

"Aren't you really angry at God about it?" she asked, sulking.

"No, I don't think it's ever been about anger. I was disappointed at first. But the more my husband and I talk about it and pray about it, the more love I have for this baby. I admit that I don't understand everything about why God is allowing it to happen this way, but my husband and I believe this will work out to be a blessing and not some kind of punishment from God. We rest in the fact that God is too wise to make a mistake, too loving to do something unkind, and too powerful to not prevent something from happening unless somehow it could bring glory to Him and blessing to us and others. And if, as you said, I seem confident and joyful, it's because my husband and I know and believe these truths about God as we handle the present and move forward toward the future."

"Well," Camilla admitted, "you may feel that way about what is going on with you, but I don't like it one bit. And I still don't think what's happening is fair."

"Tell me," Laura began, "if you don't mind my asking, what do you know about God? What are your thoughts about God? Where does God fit into all this for you?"

Camilla responded, "I know He exists, and I know that Jesus Christ is the Son of God who came to die for our sins. I used to go to church regularly, and while at church I heard about God's being holy, loving, powerful, and wise. In fact, several years ago I recognized that I was a sinner and needed God's forgiveness. So I confessed my sins to Him and asked Jesus Christ to save me. And for a while I read my Bible and prayed and tried to live the way He wanted me to live. But then I got married, and Freddie wasn't interested in going to church or anything spiritual. So I kind of followed his lead and moved away from God and the Bible and church. And now this has happened. I know I haven't been much of a Christian, but even so, I don't think I deserve this. I just can't understand why God is punishing me this way. There are a lot of other people who are a lot worse than I am, and yet they have healthy babies and a husband who loves them and is faithful to them."

Laura continued, "So you're saying that there was a time when you acknowledged your sins to God and called upon

Christ to forgive you and cleanse you from them and make you a child of God."

"Yes, I did all that, but I must admit that I haven't thought much about what it means to be a Christian for a long time. In fact, I haven't thought much about God at all until recently, when all this bad stuff started happening to me. Now, to be honest, my thoughts about God actually make me feel worse because if God were powerful and wise and loving, He certainly wouldn't allow these things to be happening to me. When I was going to church, I remember hearing the pastor preach on a verse in Romans chapter 8. I remember him saying that God promises to work all things together for good. Well, maybe He does that for others, but He's certainly not doing that for me. Sometimes I think God must keep that promise with everyone else and He makes an exception with me."

"What makes you think that?" Laura queried.

"I don't know. It just seems that way, that's all."

"You seem so sad. I'm sorry. But maybe we can support each other through this experience. What's your name, by the way?"

"Camilla."

"I'm Laura. May I tell you something?"

"Sure!"

"Camilla, what God is bringing us through is really tough. But if a person is a real believer, God gives that person what he or she needs to get that person through every trial. He's made that promise, and He will keep it. And you know what else I think: I think He put us together today for a reason. What's happened here today is not an accident.

God planned it, and He planned it for the good of both of us. We're both facing some tough circumstances. Maybe we can help each other. What would you think about the idea of our getting together like once a week to just talk? We could help each other through this, and maybe we could study the Scriptures together and pray. I think that would help me a lot. How about you?"

"Well, I don't know. I don't know a lot about the Bible—just the basics, you know."

"Maybe I can help you with that. What do you say?"

Camilla was very quiet and still for a moment. When she spoke again, tears glistened again in her eyes. But this time, the reason was that in this woman, she'd seen strength and peace that she recognized as different from her own feelings. And she realized that she wanted what Laura had. She wanted to believe that God had not abandoned her or played some kind of dirty trick on her. For the first time since she'd found out about the baby's problems, Camilla felt the tiniest glimmer of . . . what was that? She sighed when she figured it out. It was . . . hope!

"Yes," she said, with a smile. "Yes, I'd like that."

The two new friends exchanged phone numbers and promised to meet again in a couple of days. Laura even suggested having Camilla and Freddie over for dinner one night so that the guys could get acquainted, too.

Just then Tonya came to the door. "Camilla? Are you ready?"

"Yes," Camilla said. "Yes, I think I am!"

"Day by Day"

Day by day and with each passing moment,
Strength I find to meet my trials here;
Trusting in my Father's wise bestowment,
I've no cause for worry or for fear.
He whose heart is kind beyond all measure
Gives unto each day what He deems best—
Lovingly, its part of pain and pleasure,
Mingling toil with peace and rest.

Ev'ry day the Lord Himself is near me
With a special mercy for each hour;
All my cares He fain would bear, and cheer me,
He whose name is Counselor and Pow'r.
The protection of His child and treasure
Is a charge that on Himself He laid;
"As Your days, your strength shall be in measure,"
This the pledge to me He made.

Help me then in every tribulation
So to trust Your promises, O Lord,
That I lose not faith's sweet consolation
Offered me within Your holy Word.
Help me, Lord, when toil and trouble meeting,
E'er to take, as from a Father's hand,
One by one, the days, the moments fleeting,
Till I reach the promised land.

—*Karolina W. Sandell-Berg, 1865*

Reflection, Application, and Discussion Questions

1. What were Camilla's circumstances? What unpleasant things had she experienced and was she now experiencing?

2. Describe what this scenario indicates about Camilla's spiritual life before the news that the child in her womb had serious birth defects.

3. What was Freddie's response to the news about the child's having serious birth defects?

4. What was Camilla's response to the news about the child and to Freddie's threats and anger?

5. What didn't she do or think that this book indicates would have helped her to handle the difficult situation in which she found herself?

6. What are some of the things she did that only compounded her problems and facilitated her hopelessness?

7. If you were giving counsel to Camilla, what would you do or say? How would you seek to help her?

8. Have you encountered anyone in a situation similar to Camilla's?

9. Have you ever thought the way Camilla thought about the hard things you were experiencing?

10. Have you ever reacted the way she did?

11. Why do people react this way?

12. How was Laura's background different from Camilla's?

13. In what ways was Laura's background similar to Camilla's?

14. What was Laura and Josh's response to the news about the child's having serious defects?

15. What did they do that helped them to handle the difficult situation in which they found themselves? Note the various things they did that were positive influences on their thoughts, emotions, and behavior.

16. What didn't they do that some people (even Christians) do in an attempt to ease the pain and fear when confronted with a difficult situation like this? How was their response a realistic rather than a fairy-tale response? (Compare Matt. 26:38; John 11:33, 35; Rom. 12:15; 2 Cor. 7:4–6; Gal. 4:19–20.)

17. What helpful things did they specifically focus on and think about?

18. Compare what happened in the obstetrician's office between Laura and Camilla with 1 Peter 3:15.

    a. What does it mean to "sanctify Christ as Lord" (NASB), and how do Laura's actions illustrate what it means to do this?

    b. What was it about Laura that impressed Camilla and opened the door for a powerful witness to her?

    c. How do this story's events illustrate what the rest of 1 Peter 3:15 says?

19. What did Laura do and say that turned this "chance" encounter (which was actually the providence of God) into an opportunity for ministry and witness to Camilla?

Note carefully the various things she did and said in her interactions with Camilla that opened the door for future ministry opportunities.

20. When unpleasant and undesired things happen to you, do you usually do what the first part of 1 Peter 3:15 says we should do at all times, but especially when we experience suffering?

21. In those situations, what does it mean in practical terms to "sanctify Christ as Lord"? How do we do that?

22. Have you found that times of difficulty provide unique opportunities to be a witness for Christ?

   a. If so, why?

   b. If not, why hasn't that occurred?

23. Summarize what can be learned from these realistic case studies about what we should and shouldn't do when we are confronted with the apparent inequities of life.

24. Review the hymn quoted at the end of these case studies and answer the following questions:

   a. What picture of the Christian life is presented in this hymn?

   b. What comforting, encouraging, strengthening thoughts about God are mentioned in this hymn?

   c. What reasons does this hymn give for not being worried or fearful?

   d. What does this hymn tell us that God will do for us?

   e. What does this hymn suggest we must do if we are to experience the benefits it describes?

NOTES

Chapter One: The "It's Not Fair" Syndrome

1. D. A. Carson, *How Long, O Lord?* (Grand Rapids: Baker, 1990), 159–60.

2. Deborah Howard, *Where Is God in All of This?* (Phillipsburg, NJ: P&R Publishing), forthcoming.

Chapter Three: The Love of God and the "It's Not Fair" Syndrome

1. D. A. Carson, *How Long, O Lord?* (Grand Rapids: Baker, 1990), 183.

2. "And Can It Be That I Should Gain?" Charles Wesley, 1738.

3. Jerry Bridges, *Trusting God Even When Life Hurts* (Colorado Springs: NavPress, 1988), 140–41.

Chapter Five: The Omnipotence and Sovereignty of God and the "It's Not Fair" Syndrome

1. Jerry Bridges, *Trusting God Even When Life Hurts* (Colorado Springs: NavPress, 1988), 26–27.

2. Wayne Mack, *Down, but Not Out* (Phillipsburg, NJ: P&R Publishing, 2005), 216–21.

Chapter Six: The Long View of God's Justice and the "It's Not Fair" Syndrome

1. Wayne Mack, *Out of the Blues* (Bemidji, MN: Focus Publishing, 2006), 22–23, 76–77.

2. Jerry Bridges, *Trusting God Even When Life Hurts* (Colorado Springs: NavPress, 1988), 37.

Chapter Seven: Important Reminders for Overcoming and Preventing the "It's Not Fair" Syndrome

1. D. A. Carson, *How Long, O Lord?* (Grand Rapids: Baker, 1990), 243.

2. Deborah Howard, *Sunsets: Reflections for Life's Final Journey* (Wheaton, IL: Crossway, 2005), 57–58.

3. John J. Murray, *Behind a Frowning Providence* (Edinburgh: Banner of Truth, 1990), 13.

Recommended Books

Adams, Jay. *How to Overcome Evil*. Phillipsburg, NJ: P&R Publishing, 1977.

Adams, Jay. *A Theology of Christian Counseling*. Grand Rapids: Zondervan, 1979.

Bridges, Jerry. *The Joy of Fearing God*. Colorado Springs: WaterBrook, 2004.

Bridges, Jerry. *Transforming Grace*. Colorado Springs: NavPress, 1991.

Bridges, Jerry. *Trusting God Even When Life Hurts*. Colorado Springs: NavPress, 1988.

Carson, D. A. *How Long, O Lord?* Grand Rapids: Baker Books, 1990.

Charnock, Steven. *The Existence and Attributes of God*. Lafayette, IN: Sovereign Grace, 2001.

Howard, Deborah. *Sunsets: Reflections for Life's Final Journey.* Wheaton, IL: Crossway, 2005.

Howard, Deborah. *Where Is God in All of This?* Phillipsburg, NJ: P&R Publishing, forthcoming.

Lloyd-Jones, D. Martyn. *Spiritual Depression: Its Causes and Cure.* Grand Rapids: Eerdmans, 1965.

MacArthur, John. *Coming Face to Face with His Majesty.* Peabody, MA: Victor Books, 1993.

Mack, Wayne. *Down, but Not Out.* Phillipsburg, NJ: P&R Publishing, 2005.

Mack, Wayne. *Out of the Blues.* Bemidji, MN: Focus, 2006.

Mack, Wayne, and Joshua Mack. *The Fear Factor.* Tulsa, OK: Hensley, 2002.

Mack, Wayne, and Joshua Mack. *God's Solutions to Life's Problems.* Tulsa, OK: Hensley, 2002.

Packer, J. I. *Knowing God.* Downers Grove, IL: InterVarsity, 1993.

Pink, A. W. *The Attributes of God.* Repr., Grand Rapids: Baker, 2006.

Pink, A. W. *The Sovereignty of God.* Grand Rapids: Baker, 1984.

Ryle, J. C. *Holiness.* Repr., Cambridge: James Clarke & Co., 1956.

Tozer, A. W. *The Knowledge of the Holy.* New York: Harper One, 1998.

STRENGTHENING MINISTRIES INTERNATIONAL

Strengthening Ministries International exists to provide training and resources to strengthen you and your church. We as individuals and as a ministry exist to glorify God by doing what Paul and his associates did in Acts 14:21–22. Luke tells us that Paul and his associates went about preaching the gospel, making disciples, strengthening the souls of those disciples, and encouraging them to continue in the faith.

Like Paul, we are dedicated to using whatever gifts and abilities, whatever training and experience, whatever resources and opportunities we have to strengthen individual Christians and churches in their commitment to Christ and in their ministries for Christ.

And like Paul, we are attempting to strengthen the church and individual Christians in a variety of ways. Fulfilling our ministry involves conducting seminars and conferences all over the United States and in many foreign countries. It includes writing and distributing books and booklets and developing and distributing audiotapes and videotapes on numerous biblical/theological/Christian life/counseling subjects.

Fulfilling our purpose for existence, as described in Acts 14:21–22, also includes developing and sustaining Web sites:

www.mackministries.org
www.strengtheningministries.co.za
www.audubonpress.com.

On these sites you will find fuller descriptions of the various aspects of our ministry, as well as instructions about how to order materials.

Strengthening Ministries International
Mailing Address: 513 Oregon Street,
Pretoria, South Africa, 0043
E-mail: strengtheningmin@aol.com
Web site: www.mackministries.org

Wayne A. Mack (M.Div., Philadelphia Theological Seminary; D.Min., Westminster Theological Seminary) serves Christ and His church as professor of biblical counseling at Grace School of Ministry in Pretoria, South Africa. He is also adjunct professor of biblical counseling at The Master's College and teaches at the Expositor's Seminary and the Ministry Training School of the Bible Church of Little Rock, Arkansas.

Wayne is director of Strengthening Ministries International, an executive board member of F.I.R.E. (Fellowship of Independent Reformed Evangelicals), and a charter member and executive board member of the National Association of Nouthetic Counselors. He is also a member of the board of directors of the missionary agency Publicaciones Faro de Gracia, and conducts conferences and seminars in several countries.

Mack has authored more than 20 books, including *Down, but Not Out*; *Humility*; *Reaching the Ear of God*; *A Fight to the Death*; and *Your Family, God's Way*. He and his wife Carol have been married for over fifty years and have four children and fourteen grandchildren.

Deborah Howard lives near Little Rock, Arkansas, where she divides her time between writing, lectures, and nursing. Her books include *Sunsets: Reflections for Life's Final Journey* and *Where Is God in All of This?* See www.deborahhoward.net.